Mark Brown is a lecturer and consultant
in learning methods to universities,
industrial corporations and various
management training organizations. He is
also a Barrister-at-Law at the Inner Temple
and educational adviser and researcher
to the vice-chairman of the Conservative
Parliamentary Education Committee.

Memory Matters

MARK E. BROWN

SPHERE BOOKS LIMITED
30/32 Gray's Inn Road, London WC1X 8JL

First published in Great Britain
by David & Charles (Publishers) Ltd 1977
Copyright © Mark Brown 1977
Published by Sphere Books Ltd 1979

TRADE
MARK

Set in 10 on 13 pt. Baskerville

Printed in Great Britain by
Richard Clay (The Chaucer Press) Ltd,
Bungay, Suffolk

With thanks to Karen Jennings and Tony Buzan,
who made it possible for me to write this book

Contents

Introduction

Each chapter in this book begins with a 'memory pattern' which outlines the contents of the chapter.

What is a memory pattern?

A memory pattern is a diagramatic representation of the relationship between one fact and another. Its advantages over the normal linear presentation of data are twofold. Firstly, the pattern allows the brain greater creativity and freedom of association; and secondly, the pattern, being non-linear, represents more nearly than a typed list the 'organised chaos' of our mental processes.

As an aid to memory the pattern has the advantage of showing at a glance the various avenues of thought which lead off from the central theme. And therefore the brain can reassemble the lines of thought in any order it pleases, which gives much greater scope for the creative use of memory.

The memory pattern on page 14 outlines and records the content of Chapter 1. An appropriate title for the chapter is put in the centre of the pattern. Rather than using full sentences to record the information, single words are used. This type of single word is called a 'key' word and is fully explained in Chapter 2 on pp 48–50. The key words which branch from the centre are the main themes. Connected to these main themes are the secondary themes and in this way the pattern is built up. The finished pattern records all the information in a simple, linked structure. By reading the pattern you can work your way through the information presented in the chapter. Having read the chapter the pattern will help you recall the contents without reference to the text.

At the end of each chapter you will find a summary of what you have read. The purpose of this summary is to help you commit what might otherwise be a short-term memory into a long-term memory. The principles of this are discussed on pages 21–2.

Patterns are more fully explained in Chapter 3 on pp 65–72. To help you understand the principle a simple pattern is illustrated here to demonstrate how the structure develops.

Principles of the internal combustion engine

The engine is the power house of the car. Fuel is burnt to produce heat. The heat is converted into energy which turns the wheels. The fuel is normally a mixture of petrol and air.

Pistons inside the cylinders of the engine compress the mixture which is then ignited by a spark plug. As the mixture burns it expands forcing the pistons to move.

The movement of the pistons is transferred into a rotary movement to drive the crankshaft which in turn transmits power to the wheels.

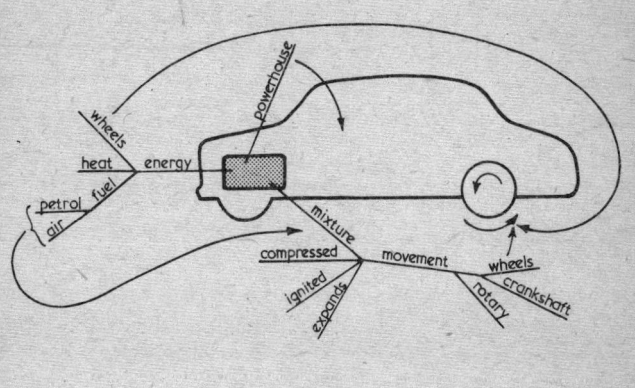

1 What is Memory ?

The definition of memory — The types of memory — The process of memory — Recall and recognition — Models of memory — Long- and short-term memory — Theories about memory — Memory transplants — The brain and its cells — Locating of memory — Summary

How do you know you remember?

If you had no memory, the question 'how do you know you remember?' would have no meaning; you would be unable to see it. A person is only able to see and recognise anything because of information stored and remembered. You relied on memory to recognise this book as a book and so to start reading it. You also relied on memory to see and recognise the sentence, the words and the letters. Finally you relied on memory to make sense of the question.

How much do you imagine a person remembers? How long would it take you to write down everything that you can remember? Would it take an hour, a day, a month or even longer? If you were to try to do this, you might start by jotting down all the words you know, then perhaps the thousands of personal memories and images that those words conjure up for you. You could then write down all the facts you know, all the experiences you have had, literally everything you can remember about anything. While writing, other memories would be triggered off. New ideas would also come to mind which would then have to be recorded. It would be a lifetime's work.

So why is it that one of the most commonly heard

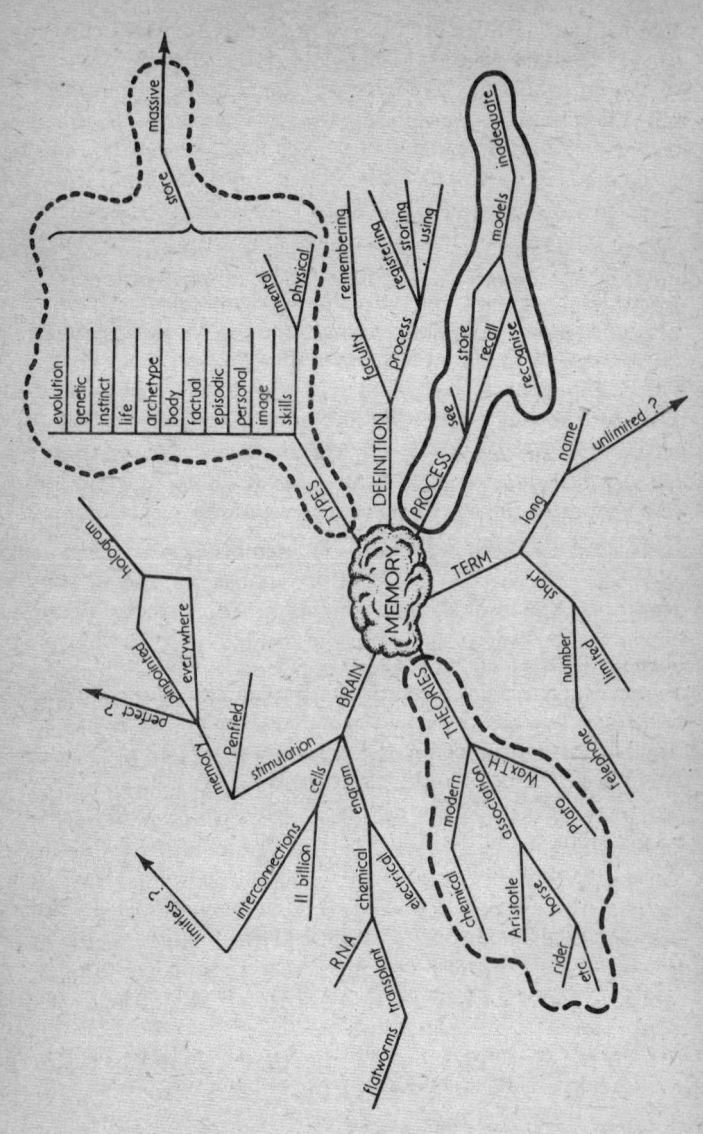

statements about memory goes something like: 'My memory gets worse all the time', or 'I've got a terrible memory for . . .'? Surely, if it could take a lifetime to write down everything you remember, it is more appropriate to say: 'I have a phenomenal memory'. Your vocabulary alone contains between ten and thirty thousand words. You have the ability to group these words in various sequences and so make different sentences with various meanings. You can form these groups into many hundreds of thousands of different meaningful sentences. This is a truly remarkable example of constructive memory. You remember places, friends, events, figures, skills and perhaps other languages. You have a mass of stored information.

It is important to realise that you do have an enormous memory capacity, since an awareness of this will automatically help in its further development. Those minor memory difficulties which you may have are not a reflection of your memory ability but of the way you are trying to commit information to memory in the first place.

What is memory?

Does memory equal every fact and experience which you have stored in a black box in a certain part of your head? Does everything you remember amount to memory? Do all your personal memories, all the facts you know and all the ideas you have stored, do all these things amount to memory?

A dictionary definition of memory is: 'faculty of remembering'. The definition of the verb to remember is given as: 'retain in the memory, not forget, recall to mind, recollect'. Both these definitions show that memory is an active process. This process can include the registering, storing and using of any stimulus recorded by an individual.

What happens when you remember an everyday event? The event is perceived, stored and later may be remembered. In this more everyday way, memory can be defined as the accumulation of everything that a person remembers. All your memories make you the individual that you are. Their uniqueness helps in creating your unique personality.

Types of memory

Some memories we are born with; others — our individual memories — begin at birth.

Evolutionary memory Mankind carries traces of the whole evolutionary process. This can be seen in the way the body is based on the general anatomical patterns of the mammal. At a molecular level the body may contain a record of the history of the earth and universe.

Genetic memory Inherited traces are carried forward through genes. These genes affect both physical and psychological characteristics.

Instinctive memory This type of memory is seen in a baby who sucks at its mother's breast or a young child who 'remembers' to cry when hurt or frightened.

Similar to instinctive and body memory is *essential life memory*. This type of memory works hand-in-hand with the nervous system. Such memory includes the brain's control of heart beat, sleep and appetite. Although these functions are often considered automatic, the brain has to remember how to control these activities.

Archetypal memory Archetypes are usually associated with the work of Carl Jung, the famous Swiss psychologist and one-time co-worker of Freud. Archetypes are elements or symbols which usually occur in dreams. They are supposedly not derived from the dreamer's personal experiences. These elements or mental forms seem to be aboriginal, innate and inherited. An archetype can thus be seen as a symbolic image; although the image has no obvious personal relevance it is argued that people may have a common fund and memory of symbolic images.

A more down-to-earth type of memory is *factual memory*, for example a person may know the date of the Battle of Hastings or the year of the first four-minute mile. This memory holds a multitude of facts, names, dates and events.

Body memory A change in the body is a record both of the events causing that change and of the change itself. A cut on the leg may leave a scar which remains as a record of the injury and the cut. A tanned skin is a record of the effects of the sun's rays on the skin. Excess fat can be seen as a record of over-eating.

Episodic memory This records episodes and provides a sense of time, and enables an individual to know that yesterday was yesterday and that today is today.

Personal memory This records feelings, emotions and ideas.

Physical skill memory Physical abilities that become fluent and automatic are often called skills. The child who remembers the muscle movement, timing and co-ordination in order to walk may be said to have mastered the skill of walking. Some fairly automatic physical movements may be seen as habits

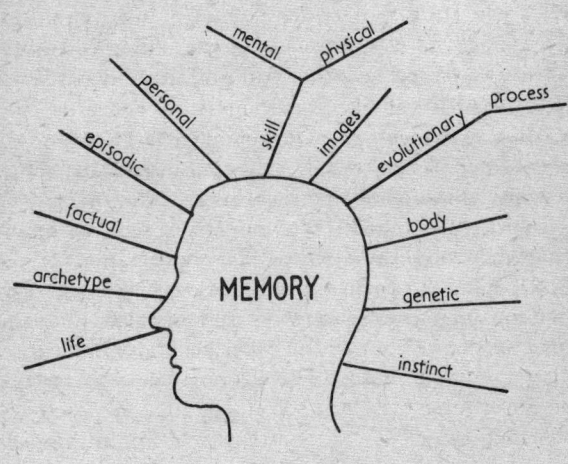

rather than skills. These may be seen as both good, for example, checking for traffic before crossing a road, or bad, biting your fingernails.

Mental skill memory You learn to count and multiply automatically, you remember letters and words so as to construct meaningful sentences without having to consciously work out each letter and word.

Image memory You are able to recall clear images of past events, friends and places. Such images can occur with crystal clarity in dreams.

Memory is, therefore, directly involved in all human activity and behaviour.

The process of memory

The process of memory or remembering can be broken down into three main stages. For example, let us suppose you look up from this book and see an eagle. The following process may take place: firstly you see the eagle, and to be able to see and recognise the eagle you have to rely on past memories. Secondly, you store the fact or images of seeing the bird. Thirdly, you will be able consciously to recall that you saw the eagle. Stage one is seeing and recognising; stage two is storing and stage three is recalling.

Sometimes, although the information has been stored, it may seem impossible to recall it. Trying to recall a fact that you usually know perfectly well can be infuriating. Some stored information, although apparently forgotten, may be recalled when the same or similar information is later repeated. Although two people may not remember each other by name they may be able to recognise immediately that they have met before. This type of experience gives rise to the expression: 'I never forget a face, but I've got an awful memory for names'.

The same experience can occur when sitting in front of a

See

Store

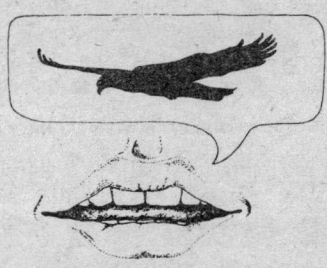

Recall

late-night television film when, after the first ten minutes, you remember having seen the film several years before.

Certain information can move from the recall to the recognition level. If a person without preparation re-sat all the examinations ever taken in his life the results in most cases would be pretty abysmal. Subsequently if the person went back to school to re-learn all the 'lost' information, he or she would constantly recognise that they had been taught the particular information before and find the re-learning a simpler task than it had been originally.

Both recall and retention are important aspects of memory. Retention may suffice for one situation while at other times you may also need effective recall. This can be illustrated by the following example: imagine that you want to travel to a friend's house and you have only been there once before. You may well feel that you will be able to find the way once you start in the right direction because when you come to a crossroads or junction or halt you will recognise the way you went before. However, if I wanted to visit this friend of yours you would not be able to tell me when to turn off or when to carry on, because you would be unable to recall the journey itself. In the first case you would be able to rely on your retention and recognition but in the second you have to be able to recall.

For recall and recognition, information has to be stored in the brain. In remembering anything a person has to retrieve the appropriate information. How does the brain know where to find a particular bit of information so that it can be recalled?

The French philosopher, Descartes, suggested that:

When the mind wills to recall, this volition causes the little gland (the pineal) by inclining successively to different sides, to impel the animal spirits towards different parts of the brain, until they come upon that part where the traces are left of the thing which it wishes to remember.

More recently, various models have been used to help try and understand memory and the way it retrieves what has been stored. Such models include filing cabinet systems and computer information banks. Although models may help in the understanding of the memory process, they have so far proved to be totally inadequate. If memories were stored like facts in a filing cabinet, how could such a system be organised so as to enable the speed and variety shown by the human mind? Even the most highly organised and cross-referenced system would be totally inadequate. Each time any information was required it would necessitate scanning-type research for the appropriate fact. The flexibility, speed and accuracy of a person's response in answering questions and remembering generally is an ability so complex that many research scientists stand in awe of the memory process.

Long- and short-term memory

If a businessman looks up a client's telephone number he will probably be able to rely on his memory and phone the number without having to read it as he dials. Later on in the day he may find that he has no recall whatsoever of the number and so will need to look it up again before 'phoning again. While some information may be remembered for only a few seconds or minutes, there is also an enormous body of information which is retained all the time. This difference gives rise to the concepts of 'short-term' memory and 'long-term' memory. A person relies on short-term memory to remember the telephone number long enough to dial it or write it down. This memory is used to remember a sentence for long enough to allow the sentence to be said and understood. On the other hand, information in the long term may be remembered for any length of time and sometimes throughout a person's life. An example of a life-long memory is the memory of your own Christian name.

Short-term memory is limited in capacity. If you try to hold a lot of information in this store you will soon have to start letting go of some of it, as the capacity becomes overfilled.

Short-term memory may become fixed in the long term. This is illustrated where a telephone number which once could be remembered only for a few moments, later becomes second nature.

Clinical evidence suggests that there is some valid distinction between short- and long-term memory. If certain parts of the brain are removed, information in the long-term store remains intact, although, however, there can be no new long-term storage. The short-term memory meanwhile remains intact.

Theories about memory

Early man had no reason to suppose that memory was located in the brain. Over two thousand years ago, memory was thought to be linked with the amount of light and dark in the body. Memory was also associated with movement of air within the body. Plato suggested a theory, still accepted by some today, known as the Wax Tablet Hypothesis. This theory suggests that memory works in the same way as an impression upon wax. Such an impression may become less clear with the passages of time.

Aristotle thought that memory was to be found in the heart. However, he accurately pointed out that our memory relies heavily on association: in other words that one fact or piece of information tends to lead on to another and then to another. If, for example, you say the word 'horse', this may trigger off the word 'rider' and that in turn the word 'riding hat' and so on. This associative process need not be so random and your associations may remain within a particular category: the word 'horse' may trigger off the idea of 'mule' and that in turn the word 'ass'.

The principle of memory by association is illustrated in the following joke: a vicar, who thought he had lost his bicycle, suddenly remembered where he had left it while preaching a sermon on the Seventh Commandment — Thou shalt not commit adultery.

As the brain became recognised as the control centre for the body, and memory was located in the brain, the theories have become more complex and, hopefully, nearer the mark. When anything is remembered, a change takes place in the brain. There is literally a brain change. It is this change that is being identified by modern research. When you remember a fact, something called a memory trace (or engram) is formed in the brain. This has to be triggered off again in order to remember the stored information. It was thought that this trace was entirely electrical in form, perhaps consisting of reverberating particles which kept the trace alive. As a comprehensive theory to explain the phenomenon of memory this has been disproved.

Although the brain works electrically, memory is not entirely dependent upon an electrical process. This has been proved by temporarily stopping all the electrical activity in the brain. It might be supposed that this would have the effect of wiping out all past memories, but, when the electrical activity is resumed memory returns unaffected.

The electrical impulse however, does play a vital role in the memory process. It appears that the initial impression or stimulus, for example of what is seen or heard, is converted into a minute electrical charge, which is finally turned into something more stable. The electrical charge seems to coincide with short-term memory.

If the brain receives a heavy blow or electric shock immediately following the learning of new information, the information will be completely lost. The blow or shock disrupts the electrical charge before it turns into a more permanent record.

So the electrical charge is just the beginning of the process. There follows a bio-chemical change in the brain which provides the more permanent memory record. This chemical seems to be tied up with ribonucleic acid — RNA. RNA is linked to DNA (deoxyribonucleic acid) which is the chemical basis of heredity. The link between memory and RNA has been shown by measuring the amount of RNA in a particular areas of the brain after a learning period. It has been found that there is a proportional increase in RNA after any learning. It seems that there are memory molecules that form chains in a particular way and register the information. These memory molecules are probably either directly connected with the production of RNA or immediately affected by that production. It is interesting to note that our genetic memory process is very closely linked to everyday memory.

Once scientists had established that more permanent memory, or long-term memory, was chemically based, research was directed to the question of whether memory could be transplanted from one creature to another. This idea is rather similar to Jonathan Swift's cephalick tincture. This tincture, when eaten on wafers, implanted knowledge in schoolboys. These transplant memory experiments usually take the following form: an animal is first taught to react in a certain way. The trained animal is then killed, its brain removed and processed. From the brain is removed an extract. This extract is injected into a live but untrained animal. The new animal is then observed to see whether or not it has learned what was 'taught' to the trained animal.

The first major experiments were carried out in the early 1950s on flatworms. A group of flatworms were taught a particular response. An extract containing RNA was taken from the bodies of the trained flatworms and injected into a group of untrained flatworms. It was found that the injected group could learn the response taught to the first group at a faster rate than a non-injected group. In this way memory seemed to be transplanted.

Experiments have been conducted which show that

memory can also be transplanted from one species to another. Chemical transplants have enabled a fear of the dark, induced into one animal, to be transferred to another animal previously unafraid of the dark.

The implications of these experiments are obviously enormous and have encouraged statements like: 'If you want to be intelligent you should eat a professor'. The argument here is that if memory can be transplanted from one animal to another, why should such a transfer not be possible between humans?

There have been many similar experiments following on from the flatworm-type findings. One such experiment attempted to show that if elderly people were fed massive doses of RNA their memories, and in fact their whole mental ability, improved. One American drug company produced a pill, designed to increase the production of RNA and so help students cram for examinations. Although neither of these last two experiments' findings are generally accepted, the possibility of memory transplants in human beings seems far from remote.

The whole memory process is based in and around the individual brain cells. The mature human brain contains about 11,000 million such cells. A small insect like an ant has only about 200 brain cells. The enormous number of cells in the human brain may be more easily comprehended by comparison with an estimate of the world's population:

—cells contained in one human brain: 11,000,000,000
—population of the world: 4,000,000,000

Each cell is less than 1/10mm in diameter — 250 brain cells would sit quite happily on the head of a pin. The brain cell, or neuron, has at its centre the cell body. Off the cell body come tentacles, from which come even smaller tentacles. This minute many-tentacled, octopus-like cell connects with other neurons through these small tentacles.

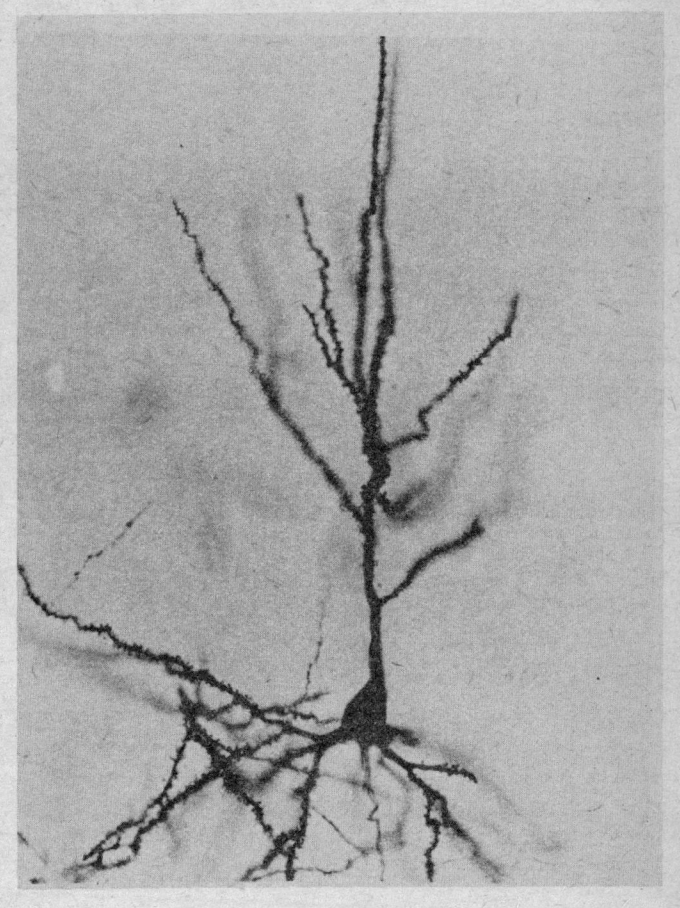

The number of possible combinations of interconnections between the 11,000 million neurons is almost beyond imagination. The capacity of the brain is recognised to be so great that one can debate the possibility that it records all experience and information received. Professor Mark Rosenzweig at the University of California has pointed out that if the brain were to absorb ten new bits of information every second of its life, from birth until death, there would still be plenty of potential for new storage.

There is evidence to show that everything we experience may be recorded. Work done in Canada by Dr Penfield shows that when a localised area of the brain is stimulated with a minute electrical charge, a whole series of events is relived as if actually real. For example, if your brain were to be stimulated in this way, say five years from now, you might actually relive every moment of today. The implication of Penfield's work gave rise to two main ideas. The first is that retention of information may be perfect, and the second idea is that memories may be pinpointed in various parts of the brain. The first idea may well be true especially in the light of the brain's complexity and potential.

The second, that is the localisation or pinpointing of memory, needs to be modified to take account of other evidence. Although Penfield showed that a particular memory seemed to live in a particular place, other research showed that any one memory might live throughout the whole brain. For example, if a rat were taught a particular ability, perhaps how to escape from a maze, according to Penfield's research, you would be entitled to argue that this ability was memorised in one spot. However, when either half of the rat's brain was removed it was discovered that some memory of the ability remained intact no matter which half of the brain had been removed. Therefore, it appeared that memory was dispersed everywhere throughout the brain. Brain damage or the surgical removal of a particular area of the brain only seemed to reduce the quality of the memory itself. Therefore, there appears to be a direct contradiction. In other words, memory is both in one particular area and almost everywhere in the brain.

An analogy used to try and help the understanding of this phenomenon is that of the hologram. Hologram simply means 'whole record'. Holography is a form of three-dimensional photography. A photograph is taken using the light waves of a laser beam. This is known as a hologram. The holographic image can be re-seen if viewed by the same laser light. This image is three-dimensional and hangs in space like a perfect stage ghost. If the glass plate onto which the photograph has been developed is smashed, any one of the broken pieces when viewed again by the same laser light recreates the whole original image. It is this characteristic of the hologram which makes it so fascinating — every part contains the whole. In a similar way a memory seems to be both confined to one area and dispersed throughout almost the whole of the brain.

Conclusion

Originally memory was essential for survival. By using memory man could modify his behaviour. He learnt to recognise and so avoid certain dangers. Often the better his memory was, the greater his chances of survival.

Today, as before, memory is essential for basic survival. Now it is also used to record information and skills as well as the code of animal survival. The excellence and organisation of a person's memory may well determine the degree of success and enjoyment he gets out of life. The involvement of memory in such activities as problem solving, creativity and every process that requires imagination stresses man's need for a good working memory.

The more memory is considered the more extraordinary it

seems. The possibility that there may be a perfect record of all experience and knowledge adds to the fascination. This feeling of wonderment is enhanced when studying people who demonstrate exceptional memory abilities, or, on the other hand, people with memory abnormalities. The complexity of the memory process has at times so baffled researchers that they conclude that memorising is an impossibility!

Memory is what makes a person an individual. The past experience of your life affects your behaviour today. Without memory you would literally have no identity — you would not know who you were. Without memory you would simply be a drifting organism bemused by momentary images and other stimuli. Without memory you would be unaware that you even exist. You would not be able to ask yourself a question like: 'To be or not to be?', since such a question would have no relevance. It can even be argued that all basic philosophical questions are asking: 'What is memory?'. Memory and identity are inexorably intertwined.

In spite of all the evidence that suggests that man has an incredibly capable memory, experience shows that it is not always as perfect as one would like it to be. A newspaper report illustrates the point: 'Japanese National railway passengers, besides leaving behind an average of 5.3 million yen (£79,000) in cash each day on trains, forgot in the year up to March 1974, 441,000 umbrellas, 396,000 articles of clothing, 72 articles of teeth and 7 boxes containing human ashes!' While this is, perhaps, rather extreme evidence of our forgetfulness, it is an annoyance that we can overcome. The following chapters will give detailed guidance on how to improve your memory and how to apply these improvements.

Summary

X Man possesses a phenomenal memory

X The process of memory: recognise and see; store and recall

X Types of memory: evolutionary, body, genetic, instinctive, essential life, archetype, body, episodic, personal, image memory, and physical and mental skill memory

X Recall and recognition: a film seen for the second time

X Memory models: inadequate

X Short-term memory: the quickly-forgotten telephone number

X Long-term memory: unlimited capacity

X Memory is electrical and chemical: memory stimulation; transplants

X Memory and the brain cell: number of potential connections

X Elusive centres of memory: one place and everywhere at the same time

X Memory matters in life and survival

2 How You Remember and Use Memory

The importance of memory — Immediate memory improvement — How you remember — Two ways of remembering,
attention and registration, note-taking — Memory and time
— Theories why you forget — Short periods, similarities and
context

The importance of memory

The importance of memory is obvious if you reflect on the
events of today. Firstly you woke up, and unlike someone
suffering from amnesia — that is loss of memory — you had
no doubt about who you are. It is obvious who you are. The
idea that you might not remember who you are seems
ridiculous. Yet you may know people who, after some sort of
blow to the head, have had difficulty in remembering certain
events or, at worse, can hardly remember anything at all.
Memory gives you a personality which you know and which
your friends also know. You need memory to have a constant
personality.

Having woken up you open your eyes and look about you.
How do you know where you are? How do you know that you
have not been kidnapped and have woken up in some strange
room? This is, again, a question of memory. 'Wait a moment',
you may want to say, 'That isn't memory as I think of it.'
Usually, when you think of memory you imagine an area of
the brain whose job it is to remember names, times, figures
and so on. This is only one small part of it. Memory is an
active process involved in every ability you have.

You may have difficulty with a very small area of memory,

for example you may always remember faces but rarely be able to put a name to them; however that only reflects an inappropriate use of memory. It is important to recognise your otherwise vast memory ability because then you will have a greater faith in this ability, tend to use it and so develop it. Special methods for developing small weak areas of your memory will be considered in the next chapter.

Finally awake, you make a determined effort to get up. You swing your legs out of bed, sit up and then perhaps stand. Again, this is an example of memory. You have remembered how to co-ordinate various muscles in particular sequence so as to get yourself out of bed — a complex manoeuvre which seems so simple — at least you hope it is simple unless you decide to reverse the procedure and get back into bed and go to sleep!

You wash, dress, eat and in every act that you perform, you call upon vast areas of information and experience. Perhaps you decide to go out for a walk. To recognise the world you constantly rely on memory. When you look at a tree, you only recognise it as such because of your flexibly recorded information. Every second you take in information through all the senses and are constantly interpreting and processing that information.

Your memory enables you to recognise what is going on and make sense of all that information. Through recognition, you learn to avoid situations, for example you try to avoid moving traffic. It is again through your memory ability that you can understand the sound and meaning of words so if someone shouts, 'Watch out, you are about to walk into a manhole!' you understand the words and avoid the danger.

When you see, hear, feel, smell, move, create, imagine, experience, talk, understand, dream, solve problems, or do anything, you rely upon previously experienced and remembered information. All the time you are sorting, recalling and cross-referencing information. As stressed

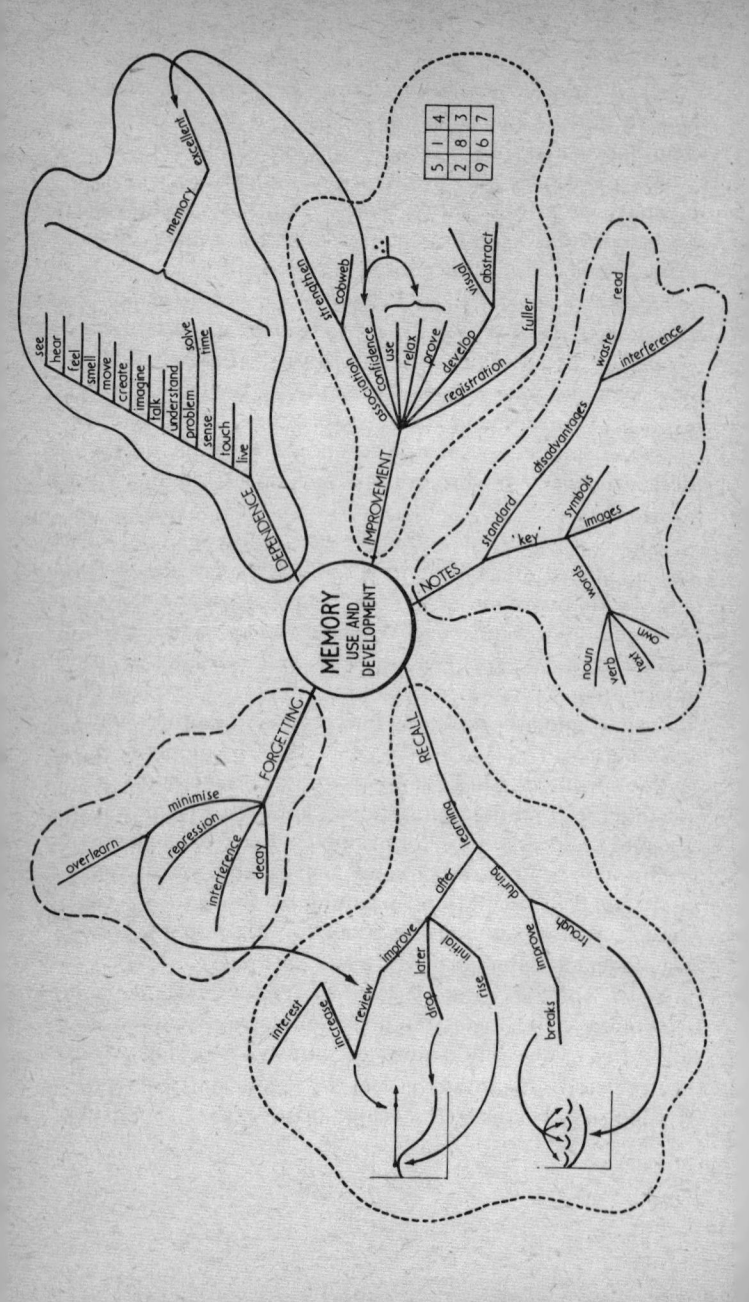

earlier, once you realise the extent to which you rely on memory it becomes more appropriate to say, 'I have a marvellous memory' rather than, 'I have a terrible memory'. Memory problems usually occur where information is fed to the brain in a poor way or perhaps not even fed in at all. Sometimes you blame your memory when in fact your memory is not at fault. For example you may claim to have a terrible memory for names, but often you will find you have not even heard the name in the first place!

Another way that you use your memory is in your sense of time. Memory gives you a sense of time, a sense of sequence. Generally what happened yesterday is a clearer memory than what happened a week ago. See for yourself. Think of yesterday and then think of last week and you will probably find that your memory of that day, if any, is very unclear. The effect of this diminishing clarity is to give you a sense of time, the feeling of time passing and an awareness of time from moment to moment.

On the other hand, there are certain events which you remember very clearly. For example, how often have you said or felt, 'It only seems like yesterday since . . .'? Sometimes certain events or places seem to be much clearer or much more precise than you would expect. For example, try and remember a vivid and happy event from your childhood and try to see it as clearly as possible. You may be able to see it very vividly indeed. Try and picture an event from yesterday and again try to see it clearly, remembering as much detail as you can. If you compare the childhood image with the image of yesterday you may find that the childhood image is even clearer than yesterday's image. You realise that there are probably many years (unless you are a very young reader) between these two events, but both are seen clearly side by side. Therefore, in a sense you are able to escape or rather to manipulate conventional time. In one sense you use this type of image memory to travel around in space. By imagining you

35

are moving quickly from one place to another, you manipulate space. You can see yourself wherever you like and travel practically instantaneously from one place to another. In this case you are using the contents of your memory in a highly imaginative way. Your imagination and memory can give you a new perspective upon the way you normally experience time and space.

To underline the extent to which we depend on memory still more, let's look at the case of an individual with a very weak memory. Zasetsky was a man who suffered severe brain damage following a war wound. He is the study of a book called *The Man with a Shattered World*, by A. R. Luria. Due to this head wound Zasetsky's memory was acutely damaged. An example of his poor memory goes as follows: Zasetsky, wanting some coal, went over to the barn to fetch some. On reaching the barn he found he had forgotten the key to open the door. And so he went back to the house to fetch the key. However, when he got to the house he could not remember why he had gone back to the house. This example may seem trivial and perhaps amusing. This is the sort of experience everyone has had at some time or another. However, Zasetsky also described his first reunion with his family after he left hospital, having recovered from his wound. Quite naturally his mothers and sisters were overjoyed to see him and greeted him with enthusiastic embraces. Although Zasetsky was perfectly aware of the welcome he was unable to respond. He had forgotten how to embrace other people! This more tragic example shows how difficult life would be with an exceptionally poor memory. Life without any memory at all is unimaginable. You would be blinded by incessant sounds, impressions and other stimuli perhaps in much the same way as a newly born child experiences the first moments of independent life.

Forgetting can give some useful insight into the nature of memory. In fact, sometimes forgetting itself is useful. If you have a friend who is killed in a car accident, your memory may dim that particular tragedy as time passes. Therefore, your memory helps alleviate painful recollections by not remembering. You may also have noticed that your memory tends to be selective. It is interesting how people tend to refer to the past as 'the good old days', illustrating that they remember pleasant rather than unpleasant experiences.

Immediate memory improvement

Although the forgetting of a painful experience may be useful, forgetfulness in general is a nuisance. How can you forget less and remember more? The importance of being confident about your memory cannot be overstressed. Believing in your own memory will have the following positive results: firstly you use it; secondly you relax when you are using it and thirdly you tend to prove to yourself that you have a good memory by using it effectively.

1 *You use it*
Next time you are introduced to somebody consider whether or not you have even heard their name. Often you find that you switched off as soon as the name was mentioned; you have not forgotten the name, you never registered it in the first place. From that experience you can either say that you are deaf or simply that you just do not hear. Hopefully, it is because you do not hear. Some people are so used to *not* remembering names that they expect to be unable to remember, and so either they do not bother to listen, or, because they know they are going to forget, they become tense and embarrassed, with the result that the name is not heard and registered clearly. If you think you have a terrible memory for names, examine what is really happening. You may well find that your memory has nothing to do with the problem and that it is really a question of a lack of concentration and general embarrassment.

2 *You relax*

By realising that you *can* remember you will become more relaxed. A relaxed attitude is important in anything you try to do. For example, in trying to thread cotton into the eye of a needle, you may find that the more you try the less you succeed. If you become very tense in your attempt to thread the cotton, your hands may begin to shake more and more until it is unlikely that you can get the cotton anywhere near the eye of the needle! The same problem occurs in learning and remembering. This can be demonstrated by experiments with other animals. If rats are trying to escape from a maze, they find their way out much faster if they are not under pressure. If the rats are especially hungry and, therefore, desperately trying to get out of the maze, they take much longer to learn the way out.

Everyone has experienced tension at school, college, at work, or at home. If you are very tense it can be practically impossible to remember and the harder you try the harder it can be. In examinations people sometimes suffer from complete memory blanks. They cannot remember a single fact during the few hours of examination, although they may know their subject perfectly. Under the stress of the examination the information just seems to disappear. So when trying to remember a fact or recall a name, do not tense up, just relax.

3 *You prove to yourself*

You find that by following this relaxed and confident approach you begin to *prove to yourself* that you have a good memory, whereas previously you may have doubted this. By seeing that you can remember, you begin to use your memory more. *You begin to prove yourself* is a key expression. Nearly everyone has a *self-proving tendency*. This means that they tend to do and achieve what they know or think they can do and achieve. If you think you have a bad memory you will tend to prove this to yourself by your performance. An example of the

38

self-proving tendency can be found with a child who is told that he is 'dumb' at a particular subject at school, say at physics. This will probably mean that if the child is not dumb at physics, it will certainly become so. The reverse of this is also true. If the child is treated with respect and praised as deserved (obviously not each time he lynches the cat or breaks the windows), that child's performance will improve by leaps and bounds. Memory responds in the same way to such encouragement. If you believe that you are bad at remembering figures, your performance will tend to prove this and you will find that your memory deteriorates because you have little faith in it and so rarely use it. If you force yourself to try and remember figures you will be tense anyway. The self-proving tendency is of general application. You will achieve what you believe you can achieve in nearly all fields of human endeavour.

To summarise so far, when you are trying to remember anything ensure that you are relaxed, be confident that you can remember, believing that your memory is getting better and better and so prove that it *is* getting better.

How you remember

An understanding of how you remember helps in itself to improve memory. In the last chapter it was suggested that association plays an important role in memory (horse — rider — riding — hat — remember?). Much of your thinking and remembering is based on a fairly simple associative process. However, how do you associate one idea with another, indeed how do you learn anything in the first place?

In watching a child develop, you observe that it learns to respond to particular stimuli. For example, a child learns to say 'kitty' when he sees the cat and so shows he associates the stimulus (the cat) with a verbal response (kitty). This basic stimulus-response idea is based on the work of the Russian psychologist, Ivan Pavlov. The simple stimulus response can probably only account for certain behaviour; for example, if you see a red traffic light you will stop; or if you are asked what four plus four make, you will know that the answer is eight. Those reactions are simple learnt responses.

When you try and solve a problem or reason out a particular argument the simple stimulus-response system is inadequate. It is probable that memorising involves both simple stimulus response and the use of more complex structures.

During the process of remembering by association you create a connection between a new piece of information and what you already know. It is, therefore, important that your association is strong and definite. When you hear a piece of information which you want to remember, you should relate, connect and associate it with as much stored information as possible. By connecting any new fact with other facts or areas of information already in your mind, you will find it much easier to understand and remember that new fact.

Information which you can relate to what you already know tends to be easier to remember. For example, if you are particularly interested in solar energy you will find it easy to absorb new detail when someone starts talking about that topic. However, if you know absolutely nothing about solar energy you will find it very difficult to make any connections at all; even though you may want to try and remember, you will find it difficult because you have too few links or connections.

To picture what is going on in the mind when one idea connects with another, imagine a cobweb, with all its complex interweaving. See this cobweb with similar cobwebs placed under it in a pile so that you have a solid mass of cobwebs, all levels interlinking with each other. This sort of network would represent only a small area of your brain. Each little strand in this analogy represents an experience or piece of information

40

stored. If a new piece of information is to 'stick' you have to make as many connections as possible between the new piece of information and every relevant, stored strand in your mind. Because you have made many connecting strands the new fact is unlikely to be lost, since it is associated with many other facts. If one connection or strand breaks you will still have several strands to support the fact, in other words by which to remember it. The new fact takes up this very related stand as part of the cobweb. The whole cobweb grows and becomes more interlinked every day. Because the brain is at work all the time the whole cobweb is changing, developing and reconnecting all the time.

By forging many connections with new ideas you also help the integration of that information. This means you will acquire a fuller, richer, more rounded mental perspective.

It is easier to be interested and remember something if you

can relate to it. Where you have information (memory) you tend also to have interest. Think about the things which interest you, and you will probably find you have quite a store of information and personal experience (these are basically the same, experience is usually living information and therefore easier to remember). Take a child who just cannot seem to remember one fact in history. (Unfortunately he may be described as a slow learner and become such, again demonstrating his self-proving tendencies.) Yet this child may be a mine of sporting facts and dates. What is the difference? He probably finds it difficult to make connections with history because he has no information. He may also see history as irrelevant and therefore he cannot make relevant associations. He may become bored and probably stops paying attention which obviously is not going to help his memory or teacher relationships — and he starts 'daydreaming'. While day-dreaming he is simply linking up connections in his head, but during a history lesson he is unable to extend a thread of his memory cobweb out to a fact because he has no similar information. However, if he were taught the history of football he would literally throw out his cobweb threads, and suck up facts, his head strained forward with thirsty attention, even contributing to the information. Simply a question of connections!

It may all seem a little too simple to say information means interest and vice versa. People do not necessarily become interested in things which relate to their experience as a very young child. However, an unusual example of this happening was reported recently: it concerned the gardeners who work in the Royal Gardens — most of whom had names of trees, shrubs or plants! From early childhood they had found connections between their names and plants and therefore a general interest developed. Although not as clearly cut as this there is also a tendency for children to follow the same sort of profession as their father or mother.

And so to summarise so far. Whenever you are trying to remember be confident, be relaxed and try to relate the information in as many ways as possible to what you already know and understand. Whenever you find you have little interest in something, by encouraging as many connections as possible, you will find you can develop a greater interest. The next time someone talks about that topic you have a definite strand of your cobweb to connect to that fact and secure it to your cobweb. You begin to be *interested*. Furthermore, with interest comes greater motivation. Memory begins to become effortless and automatic.

Two ways of remembering

Everyone is familiar with the difference between visual and abstract memory. A memory of a place is visual: the memory of an idea is abstract. You can easily demonstrate this for yourself; try to remember what the front of your house looks like. You will have no difficulty in forming a fairly clear image. On the other hand, if you are trying to remember a particular philosophical argument or theory, images may be non-existent. Your thinking, understanding and remembering is more abstract in this case, and more orientated towards abstract meaning. Some people find that they think almost entirely in a visual way while others think in a more abstract way.

Children generally have a more vivid type of visual memory. They may have thousands of colourful images whereas adults have a more abstract and verbal type of memory. Adults still use images, but to a lesser extent. A simple way to demonstrate the tendency towards abstract/visual thinking and memory is to try to recall a person's face. The person with the more visual type of memory will remember someone's face rather as though they actually see it. The person with the more abstracting type of memory may tend to remember verbal characteristics and particular features which fit into established categories and classifications.

Very often you may think you are using only one type of memory when in truth you are relying on both. For example, try and remember the following numbered square:

5	1	4
2	8	3
9	6	7

Having remembered the square, write it out without referring back. You will find that it is quite easy to do. However, again, without looking back at the numbers, write out the same pattern, but this time start with the number which is in the bottom right-hand corner and continue from there. What do you find in trying to do it this way? Probably the test is more difficult. This illustrates that you are not only using your visual ability because if that were so it should be just as easy to write out the sequence in any order. The test shows that you have adopted some form of order or sequence in your remembering. You have imposed a pattern or structure on the numbers, relying upon your more abstract type of memory and thinking ability.

When you rely upon meaning, principles, categories, or existing 'knowledge structures', you will often be using a less visual type of memory. Quite often you will use existing principles and structures and 'fit in' the new information within those principles. For example, if you were asked to remember the following letters in any sequence — ISEIEKHTISRLEIITSA — it would be difficult to remember them in that particular form. However, if you assembled those letters into the sentence, 'It is easier like this', it would be much easier to remember. In constructing a sentence from those letters you have relied upon existing categories and structures — that is your ability to make meaningful sentences from a string of letters.

By imposing order or giving a pattern to information you take a great deal of strain off your memory. Obviously, it is easier to remember the sentence, 'It is easier like this', than the string of letters. By providing meaning or order you take the strain off short-term memory and in fact also make the task easier for long-term memory. Your short-term memory has difficulty in remembering a lot of information. You can hold about seven pieces of information without having to let any of it go. These pieces of information can either be simple numbers or seven complex ideas. Providing you understand each idea separately, these seven ideas, although obviously containing much more information than seven simple digits, can be just as easy to remember as a seven-figure combination. Whenever you can make a meaningful whole of any information, your short-term memory will automatically find it easier to cope. Your long-term memory also stores information more easily if it is understood.

The more visual type of memory tends to decrease as you become older. This may be partly due to the fact that visual memory is not encouraged in education whereas it can be developed hand in hand with the more abstract type of memory. A child will often look at a wall or the ceiling before answering a question. The reason the child does this is because he is trying to project a mental image of the answer and will therefore look towards the least distracting background. Unfortunately this quite natural reaction is often mistaken for lack of concentration. By developing both types of memory together you automatically improve the whole process. Throughout this book you will find ways of increasing your visual-memory ability.

Attention and registration

Attention is vital for full registration, and both are necessary if something is to be remembered. People who claim to have bad memories for certain types of information never register the information initially. Obviously, you remember more and register more if you pay undivided attention. You want a clear and precise record and to do this you need to be able to perceive more clearly. Clear perception and full attention go hand in hand. If a person pays little attention, initial registration is bound to be weak. A person who is depressed and feels that the world has little to offer, pays minimal attention. Such a person may not even be able to remember much detail from the day before.

Clear perception is like full understanding or comprehension — to see a picture clearly is similar to understanding an idea clearly. The stronger your perception and understanding the stronger the connections being made in your mind. And so, how can a person perceive as clearly as possible? If you are looking at a picture, what is the best way to approach it? Firstly you want to be able to get a good overall view. You want to try and get a general impression of the picture. Having obtained a general impression you then want to start having a look at the detail. You might pay special attention to colour, texture, shapes and structures and so on. Finally, having scrutinised the picture, you then want to regain a good overall impression. At the last stage you try to see how the picture works as a whole and how all the detail fits into that whole. Generally, whenever you are perceiving anything, pass from the whole to the detail and back to the whole.

A good way to check the clarity of your perception is to repeat or reproduce what you have observed. In the case of a picture, you can reproduce what you are looking at by painting, drawing or sketching. Equally, you can make a mental sketch of anything that you see. This idea of reproduction applies to all forms of perception. By playing a musical instrument you enhance your musical awareness and memory; if you cook you enhance your awareness and memory of taste; through pottery you enhance your feeling and memory of touch and shape. Practice of any skill or ability will help your awareness and memory.

When you are faced with new information, try to repeat it mentally in your own as well as the original terms. Dealing with information from a different and personal angle automatically helps you understand and grasp that subject and forces you to make your cobweb connections. Through the reproduction of information you are also automatically putting it through the mental machinery; you are processing that information.

Some people think of their brain as a static container rather like a dustbin for the disposal of facts — lift the lid to fish out a fact; if it is not there it is probably because it has rotted away — or even believe that their dustbin gets full and to absorb a new fact they have to throw out an old one!

It has already been shown that your longer-term memory capacity, for all practical purposes, is limitless. Furthermore, the brain is never static, it is always at work. When you remember a fresh piece of information you automatically process the information. A fact never simply arrives and takes up residence! You have to relate to that fact, connect many possible associations to it, absorb it fully, categorise it, re-categorise it, sub-categorise it, cross-reference it many times over, and so on. All the links are stronger if you process the information by reproducing it, either by simply thinking about it or by actually repeating the information. And so, when you finally understand something, repeat it to ensure that it sticks in the memory.

Earlier you saw that you perceive and understand new information by relying upon what you have already stored.

47

You can understand this sentence and recognise your surroundings because of information you have stored. And so while perception and understanding help memory, perception and understanding are also dependent on memory. Memory, perception and understanding can therefore be seen as part of a single process.

Note-taking

Can you write down five sentences that I have used so far in this book, each containing more than ten words, and write them down perfectly, word for word? Undoubtedly not. However, you can probably remember five points that I have made in this book — at least I hope you can! The point that must be stressed here is that very rarely does anyone remember a lecture, a book, or even their own notes in full sentence form. People tend to remember both ideas and facts in a very succinct or 'key' type of mental shorthand. Memory is largely made up of key images, key symbols and key words. You want to use these key forms, especially key words, when making notes.

The effect of using these key words when noting is that you greatly reduce the volume of notes recorded. This means that there is less to read back and therefore more time to commit the information to memory.

How do you know which words make good key words? Make sure that the key word contains all the information that you want to store so that when you come across that key word again it triggers back the original information. For memory purposes main recall words tend to be verbs or nouns. The word can be one from the text, but it is often a good idea to put your own interpretation upon the text and use your own word. If an image comes to mind, rather than a word, then use the image because the image will be more memorable. You may feel that your ability to draw images, or draw at all, is so bad that the image will not help you. In fact, the reverse is true. By drawing terrible images you will find them to be incredibly memorable!

Whenever you need to remember some detailed information, take notes in key form. You want to try and use one key word, image or symbol for each idea or fact that you wish to put to memory. You will find that you need to have good comprehension of the material to be noted before you can choose or think up an appropriate key note. These key notes, therefore, help your memory in two ways: firstly this method of note-taking produces notes in a more digestible form and, secondly, by forcing you to find the right succinct key you forge strong memory connections.

Some people feel that unless they take full, standard notes, they will lose some information. For immediate recall purposes the reverse is often true. If you take long, full notes, which may have taken half-an-hour to make, it will take you fifteen minutes to read back through them. Having read through the notes you then want to commit the information to memory. Because you do not remember in full sentence form, but in a more key form, the non-key words actually hinder your memory.

To give you an example of key notes the above passage on notes itself can be key worded as follows:

> To remember — note
> Memory not sentences
> Use key word, symbol, image
> Effect, read, less
> Verbs, nouns
> Text or own
> (Even) bad images memorable
> Comprehension needed
> Full notes interfere memory

Your key words will not necessarily be the same as mine, or

anybody else's. The way to check your key notes is to ensure that each word triggers back exactly the original information.

Memory and time

A major factor which everyone knows affects memory, is time. Usually time seems to work against memory. You will have experienced this as facts fade with time. Time can, however, be used to help memory. Imagine that you attend a talk on a subject in which you are only moderately interested. The talk lasts for two hours. At the end of the talk you try and jot down as much as you can remember about what was said. You will tend to find that your memory performance in this situation can be graphed as follows:

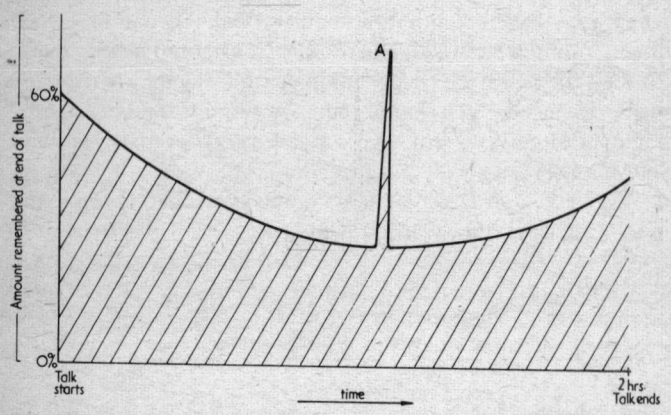

You can see that you remember most from the beginning and almost as much from the end, but there is a large loss of information during the middle, represented on the graph by the deep trough. The graph represents memory performance during a learning period and not your comprehension during

50

the talk, which may be very high throughout. Even with a high comprehension level, your memory performance will still tend to be as shown on the graph.

The high point 'A' on the graph represents a piece of information which you have remembered easily — because it was repeated, personal, humourous, or for some other reason outstanding, and does not therefore fit into the overall shape of the graph.

You obviously want to reduce this trough effect. The way to do this is to shorten the learning period. If, for example, you are revising for an exam, give yourself shorter learning periods to reduce the trough effect. The trough increases in depth the longer the period and lessens in depth the shorter the period. A period of twenty to forty minutes is best.

The effect that you are aiming to achieve can be graphed as follows:

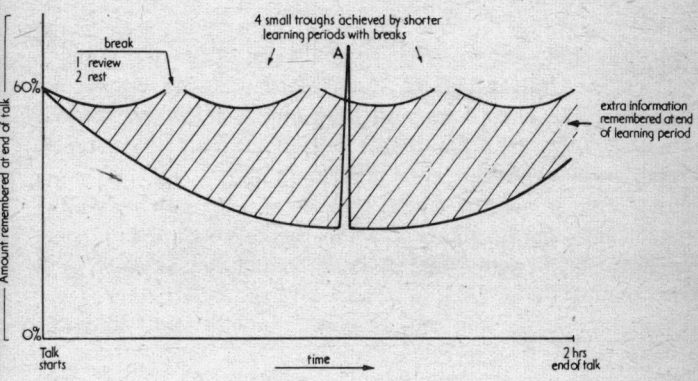

By breaking up the memory or learning period and taking time off every twenty to forty minutes you can remember all the extra shaded area. Before giving yourself a break, review and consolidate what you have covered so far and then rest, for two to three minutes. During the break do not read or start

51

any other form of learning. You will find that these breaks give you better recall of what you have covered and so you will be better equipped to understand the next block of information. After two hours' learning, even with breaks, you will probably be in need of a much longer rest and it is a good idea to have a complete change of activity. The Greek ideal of everything in moderation is a good one.

Taking breaks will also help your comprehension. You will be able to remember more of what you have learned and therefore you will find it easier to grasp and understand new information.

A break is just as important for adults as it is for children. While a five-year-old will generally be able to follow a talk for about five minutes without losing concentration, and a twenty-year-old for twenty minutes, that is about the limit and it does not follow that a sixty-year-old can concentrate for sixty minutes.

The next step is to hold on to the information for as long as possible. Let's suppose that you have just finished listening to a lecture: how much of that information do you retain immediately afterwards and how much is lost twenty-four hours later? Again, you can represent general performances on a graph. There are two surprising things about this graph: first, shortly *after* the end of the talk you actually remember more than at the moment when the talk stopped. Second, over the next twenty-four hours you may forget as much as 80 per cent of the original information remembered. This is why many people see remembering as a hopeless task, and why they say they have terrible memories.

You know from your own experiences it is easier to remember something if you have gone over it, that is, reviewed it. People who are good at telling jokes are good at it because they are constantly reviewing their repertoire. In the same way, the person who says he is bad at telling jokes rarely, if ever, tells them and, therefore, does not review any

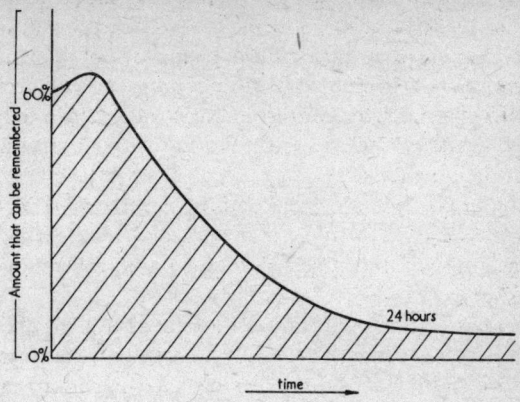

jokes and so probably could not remember any if he should want to tell one! This creates a vicious circle: the person then thinks he has a bad memory for jokes and so stops trying to remember them in the first place. Things which you remember easily are often matters that you talk about and think about, in other words, they are areas which you automatically review.

When your remember something there is a brain change which is called a memory trace or engram. To ensure that this trace is available for recall at any time, it helps to review it, in the same way that you make a muscle strong by using it. Your aim is to make sure that the thread of memory does not break.

You should review information at the time when your memory is at its peak which is a few minutes after you stop learning or remembering anything. By spending just a few minutes after a learning period you can save most of that 80 per cent loss. You will also need to review the information at later times. A good programme for reviewing information is as follows: firstly a few minutes after the learning period, then twenty-four hours later, then a week later, then a month later.

Each time you catch your memory before the information starts to fade.

All the necessary reviews are represented on the graph:

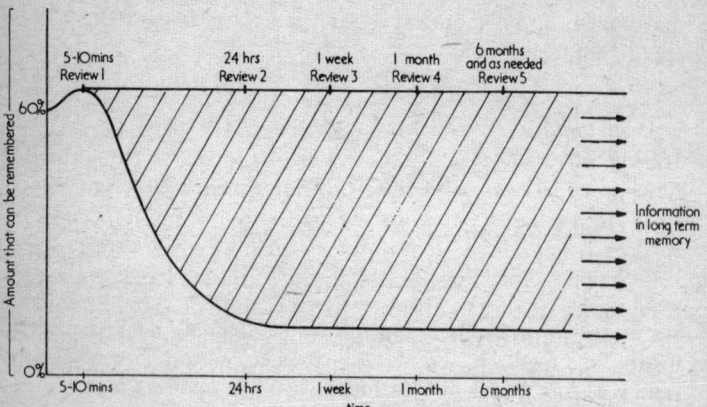

Often you will find that you are reviewing naturally through thinking and talking about ideas. However, to make absolutely sure of remembering, it is a good idea to review at regular intervals, as suggested on the graph. All these reviews will transfer the information into your long-term memory, and make it as easy to remember as your own name!

Questions

1 *Isn't it all a bit of an effort?*
I can see how you might think that. Try looking at it in terms of investment. If you work for an hour and want to remember that hour's worth of information, providing you have used key words, it will take you fifteen minutes to do all five reviews.

That means that you will have all the information stored away for life by working for one and a quarter hours. On the other hand, if you work for just one hour with no breaks, twenty-four hours later you may only have 20 per cent left. By the end of the week, you will remember even less. So to answer your question: I think I should say, 'Isn't it a waste of your effort, if you do not review?'.

2 *Are all the reviews necessary?*
If I say 'no' a lot of people heave a sigh of relief and think they have an excuse never to review! The answer is best put like this: the earlier reviews are the most important, especially reviews 1 and 2. The review times suggested are meant to be used as guidelines and, especially with the later reviews, *you* need to decide the best review times. Often you will find that the first two or three reviews, if properly done, are sufficient. This is because you automatically review much information by thinking and talking about it.

3 *Can you sum up why you use key notes, and how you review them?*
The idea of review is to see that you have remembered all the information that you want. So if you have been taking down notes, make sure that you can repeat all the recall key words. If your key words are good recall words you will find that one word will remind you of the next and so on. You will also find that your choice of key words improves with practice. You will realise immediately if you have selected a bad key word because the information will be hard to remember.

To review you take a piece of paper, and make sure that you can copy from memory all the key words. As your memory improves you will be able to run through the words in your head; if you cannot remember one, simply refer back to your notes. Notes that are not in key form are practically impossible to review. The reason for this is as follows:

* If you have taken long-hand — that is non-key — notes it takes too long to read them all back.

* Even if you do have time to read all the information back, because the notes are not in concise memory form, you cannot find the key words to commit to memory.

* Even if you do find the key words, the mass of other information will be a handicap to your memory of the recall key words.

* You will have discovered for yourself, if you have not been taking key-word notes, that your comprehension is usually much lower than when key notes are used.

4 *What are the effects of a review system?*

Firstly, you find that you can quickly recall any information that you have reviewed. Whatever your reason for wanting to remember something — whether it be for pleasure or out of necessity — you find that you can recall the ideas almost immediately. For the first time you begin to feel you really can remember; instead of behaving like a sponge, absorbing information which is squeezed out again after a few hours. The effect of this upon your interest is most marked. Because of the relationship between memory and interest, as your store of information grows, you will find that you become interested in ideas for which you showed little concern previously.

If someone is talking to you about something outside that store, you cannot make connections and therefore it is hard to become interested. If your body of knowledge is larger it is easier for you to see the relevance of the information so you will tend to pay more interested attention, make connections and so remember easily. This interest leads to new interest and quickly the whole process snowballs.

At this point it is worth reflecting on the one-subject approach to learning which you probably experienced at school. By reviewing information you will quickly discover that all subjects are inter-related. It is interesting to note that elderly people who keep mentally active and acquire a large amount of information, whether factual or in the form of experience, usually have very alert minds, and find interest and mental stimulation right into their old age. Conversely, an old person who has little information finds it difficult to relate to what is going on, may feel alienated and mentally sterile.

Why do I ever forget?

It is important to realise that the word 'forget' tends to be used in two ways: either it can mean that you cannot remember immediately, for example, when you cannot remember a friend's name but remember it shortly afterwards; or, the other meaning, where you literally do not seem capable of ever bringing the information back to mind.

You have seen that very often forgetting is caused by very poor initial registration with subsequent lack of strong connections, but there are situations when even though you have remembered quite clearly you simply cannot seem to remember later — in this situation what has happened?

Imagine you have learned a poem today. It only took a short time to master the poem and you can now repeat it perfectly. Tomorrow you may be able to remember only some of the lines of the poem and perhaps in a year's time you may only be able to remember one or two lines. Many people imagine that the information has simply decayed with time. Memories do not decay. (Remember from Chapter 1 how Penfield's research showed that many memories, although not available for recall, are stored permanently.) One theory that explains why forgetting occurs is the theory of interference. This idea is simply that what you learn is very often disturbed or displaced by what you subsequently do to that learning. You will have noticed that if you remember or learn something just before going to sleep you can remember the information quite well the next morning. Sleeping does not involve much new activity and so there is a minimal amount of interference.

Another explanation centres around repression. This idea suggests that you unconsciously repress certain things, certain experiences in your life, because you do not want to remember them. In extreme cases, people are totally unable to remember certain events or certain periods of their lives, especially if these events or periods were particularly unpleasant. In this type of situation a person can be helped to remember through hypnosis. Under hypnosis a person tends to be more open to suggestion and so, by using free association, the person can work his or her own way back along the various connections and associations of the memory framework to the original event. To some extent everyone represses certain types of information. This was illustrated in Chapter 1 by the way that you tend to remember the more pleasant experiences of your life rather than the unpleasant. In many ways memory repression is a perfectly healthy instinct.

Very few people can remember much information from early in their life. Why is it so difficult to remember our very early childhood experience? Freud suggested that this was because our motives in early years are selfish and quite often sexually orientated and that therefore the memories are repressed. Another possible explanation is that much of what we remember as adults is dependent upon structures of knowledge developed later in life. A child has set up very few structures, has very few organised ideas and, therefore, does not make associations in the same way an adult does. An adult's memory is also verbal, whereas a young child's has very little, if any, verbal ability; it may therefore be difficult to translate the world of childhood experience into verbal terms. A child remembers a lot of information but the methods he remembers it by are very different from the methods he uses as an adult.

The main reason why forgetting occurs appears to be that information interferes with other information. So when you take breaks during learning you want to make sure that your rest activity is as different as possible from the original learning. This minimises the effect of interference. Furthermore, interference is never as marked, in other words, your memory is always better, if you overlearn information in the first place.

Another question quite often asked is whether, if interference is minimal while you are asleep, it is a good idea to study just before going to bed. The answer is a qualified yes; the problem is that it tends to be more difficult to commit information to memory later in the day when you are probably more tired. The rather unsatisfactory conclusion is that the best way to learn is to get up and work for a short time and then go back to sleep! A more practical way to help overcome interference is to learn well in the first place and then review the information.

Short periods, similarities and context

Whenever you are trying to remember or learn anything, it is always better to work for a short period of time than a long period of time. Providing that you have comprehension within a short period, your memory will always do better. And so, whether you need to learn a short poem or a mass of information, it is more advisable to spread it over short periods of time fairly regularly — over several days if necessary — than it is to concentrate it into just one long period. In fact, even if the total learning time is less over a longer period, that is often better than spending more time in one extended session.

When you are trying to remember, impose an order, structure, or pattern on the information which helps you absorb and remember it. For example, the letters ISEIEKHTISRLEIITSA, were easier to remember as 'It is easier like this'. Whenever you are faced with a list of information

59

you help your memory by looking for similarities in the facts. However, if the information is already very similar in context, you need to stress the dissimilarities between the individual facts and so highlight each piece of information so that it is different enough to be remembered.

The context, that is, the situation in which you learn information, also affects memory. For example, you may well have experienced meeting somebody from your office while on holiday abroad; in this situation a lot of people find it impossible to immediately remember the person's name. Because the person is out of context they cannot make the appropriate associations or connections, whereas they would automatically remember the person's name if they had met at work. If a certain piece of information is out of context, it can be particularly hard to trace or name. In this situation it is much easier to recall if you imagine yourself in the surroundings where you first learnt the information. This is the reason why children perform better if examinations are taken in the room where they were taught.

The 'morning after' memory lapses are an example of how the physical context affects memory. Imagine you drove to a party last night and had too much to drink while you were there. However, before you got completely drunk, you realised that you ought not to drive. You also knew that if you had much more to drink you would not know that you were unfit to drive! So, you decided to hide your keys in order to make it impossible for you to drive home later on. You did this, carried on drinking, could not find the keys and so finally walked — or staggered — home! Today you started searching for the keys. You will find it much easier to remember where you actually put the keys by getting drunk again — that is, putting yourself in the same situation again. The point to recognise is that whenever you are trying to remember anything, try and put yourself back in the original context where you received the information or whatever it is that you are trying to recall. By doing this you will find that the context gives you extra clues and associations and so helps you to remember.

And so to summarise the ways to help your memory . . .

Summary

X Realise how excellent your memory actually is

X Start using your memory

X Relax when you remember and recall

X Prove to yourself how good your memory really is

X When remembering, try and make as many connections with the new piece of information as possible

X Feel motivated to remember, realising how memory affects interest

X Ensure full attention when remembering

X Ensure clear perception and understanding when remembering

X Try to reproduce, repeat and review the information or experience

X When noting information make it as key as possible

X When learning or remembering over a period of time take short breaks of 2–3 minutes every 20–40 minutes. You need to take a substantial break every 2 hours

X The best time to review notes is a few minutes after you have stopped working. The information then needs to be reviewed several times over the next few months. However, do remember that to an extent you are always reviewing information simply by thinking about it or talking about it

X When you are trying to commit items of very similar information to memory, stress the differences as well as the similarities

X When trying to remember a fact that you cannot recall, try and put yourself back in the original context

3   Memory Improvement

Difficulty in remembering is not a reflection upon your memory ability and brain but rather indicates that you have been feeding your memory in an inappropriate manner. Most people would like to be able to remember much more information than they actually do. There are many facts, and ideas and knowledge generally, which, from schooldays onwards, you would like to keep permanently stored. Although nobody wants simply to stuff his head full of facts, like a filing cabinet or esoteric reference library, there is a mass of information that you do come across that would be useful if you had it at your fingertips. And, furthermore, when you consider how memory affects interest, it is obviously an advantage to keep more information at the recall level.

Some people make the mistake of thinking that they should try not to remember too much because they will not be able to think straight! This idea is based upon the image of the brain as a dustbin. You can absorb much more information and, with training, recall it at will. This extra information does not clutter your conscious mind — it is simply available when you want it. Realising your potential, your memory potential, you will probably want to start using and developing it straight away.

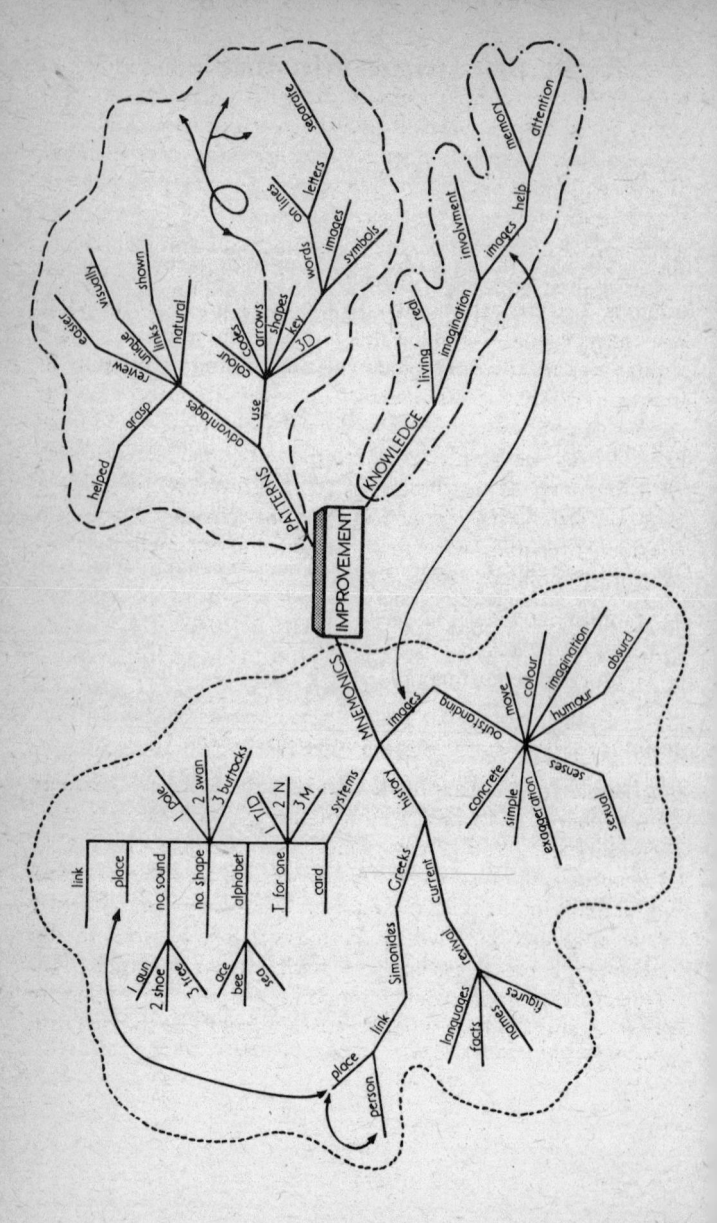

When you try to increase or improve any ability you can help yourself by simply using it. If you want to remember a poem, for example, you will find that with practice and after having learned several poems, your learning and memory ability will have improved. However this increase will not continue indefinitely. After a certain amount of practice you will improve no more unless your method of learning changes.

You might find that, to begin with, it takes you twenty minutes to learn a particular length of poem. With practice you may be able to reduce this to fifteen minutes to learn a similar poem. However, you will find that it is difficult to improve on that performance. The way to improve your memory in this situation is to consider the method you are using for learning and remembering a poem. The problem with memory is nearly always a question of method, a question of how the memory is fed. This chapter is going to consider three main ways in which to feed your memory so as to help it. These are:

1 Memory patterns
2 Living knowledge
3 Memory systems/mnemonics

Memory patterns — theory and application

The key form of noting is the best way to record information for memory and recall. How can this method be improved even further? You know that your memory is highly associative and inter-linking. Therefore, it is a good idea if you can actually try and reproduce that linking network. Instead of writing in lines when preparing information to be remembered, create a visual interlinking structure which more naturally represents your mind and memory on paper. A simple example of this type of structure looks like the diagram over the page.

65

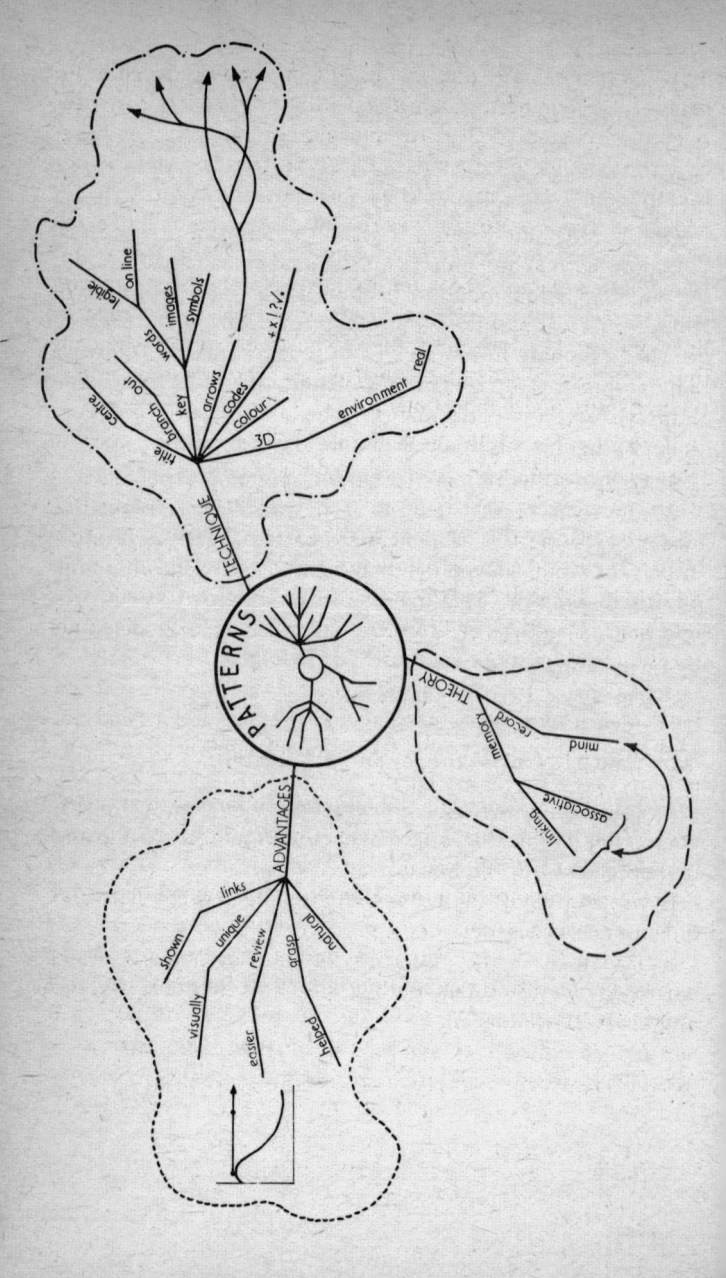

PATTERNS

TECHNIQUE
title
centre
branch out
key
images
words
on line
legible
Symbols
arrows
codes
colour
3D
environment
real
+ x / ? /.

ADVANTAGES
links
shown
unique
visually
review
easier
natural
grasp
helped

THEORY
mind
record
memory
associative
linking

This pattern explains the use and theory behind patterns in general. By looking through it you will find that it is easier to read and understand the written explanations. After you have read the explanations turn back to this pattern and you should find that all the information is held within it in key form.

This memory pattern shows the links between one idea, or one fact, and another. It is visually different and this is an immediate advantage because, by having a unique structure, it is far easier to remember than the usual pages of standard linear notes. The form also allows you to grasp the whole of the subject by enabling you to see the various inter-relationships and connections.

To explain more fully the techniques of the pattern:

1 The title is written in the centre of a plain piece of paper.

2 The main points stem out from the centre. Always use single key words in the memory pattern. The next most important points link off the main points, and then sub-points off those points etc. This tree-like structure grows as you add information and you will notice that you have to understand the information before you know where to place it correctly.

3 Make sure that your handwriting is very legible — it is a good idea to use separate, clear and rounded letters and not ordinary handwriting — so that you can see and read the pattern easily.

4 You should write the individual key words on the line. If you do not do this the pattern becomes visually confusing and therefore less easy to remember.

5 Use arrows, codes and colours to help you to relate and link up the various ideas in the pattern.

6 Try to make the pattern as original as possible. Each pattern should be visually unique, since it is easy to remember anything that is unusual.

7 Do use images or symbols if you feel these are more appropriate than words. If an idea or fact is naturally seen by

you as an image — use it. Do not use a verbal tag instead, it will only slow up your recall.

8 Try to inject some realism into the pattern. It is much easier for the mind to remember its real environment, that is, its three-dimensional environment. So make your patterns three-dimensional by using colour, shapes, structures and images.

The pattern based on the following text shows how an area of information can be held in one easily remembered visual structure. This is only one example of a memory pattern. You should try and develop your own individual style.

Michelangelo

This pattern records the life and achievements of Michelangelo, the world-famous artist. He was born near Florence in 1475. His father, who was a magistrate, opposed Michelangelo's desire to become an artist. Nevertheless, at the age of thirteen, he began his apprenticeship under the famous Florentine artist, Ghirlandaio. Michelangelo was influenced by Ghirlandaio's frescoes and by Masaccio and Giotto, whose works he copied as part of his apprentice training.

To further his studies he then went to the Medici Garden, a centre sponsored by the patron, Lorenzo de Medici, for aspiring artists.

His first major piece of sculpture was completed in 1500 in Rome. This was the *Pietà* in St Peter's, and is recognised as a remarkable study of human anatomy.

In 1501 he returned to Florence as a famous artist. It was here that he completed one of his greatest masterpieces — the *David* — in 1504. He started work on the *Twelve Apostles* in 1503, which he never completed.

Michelangelo was commissioned by Pope Julius II to work on his tomb in Rome which in its original conception

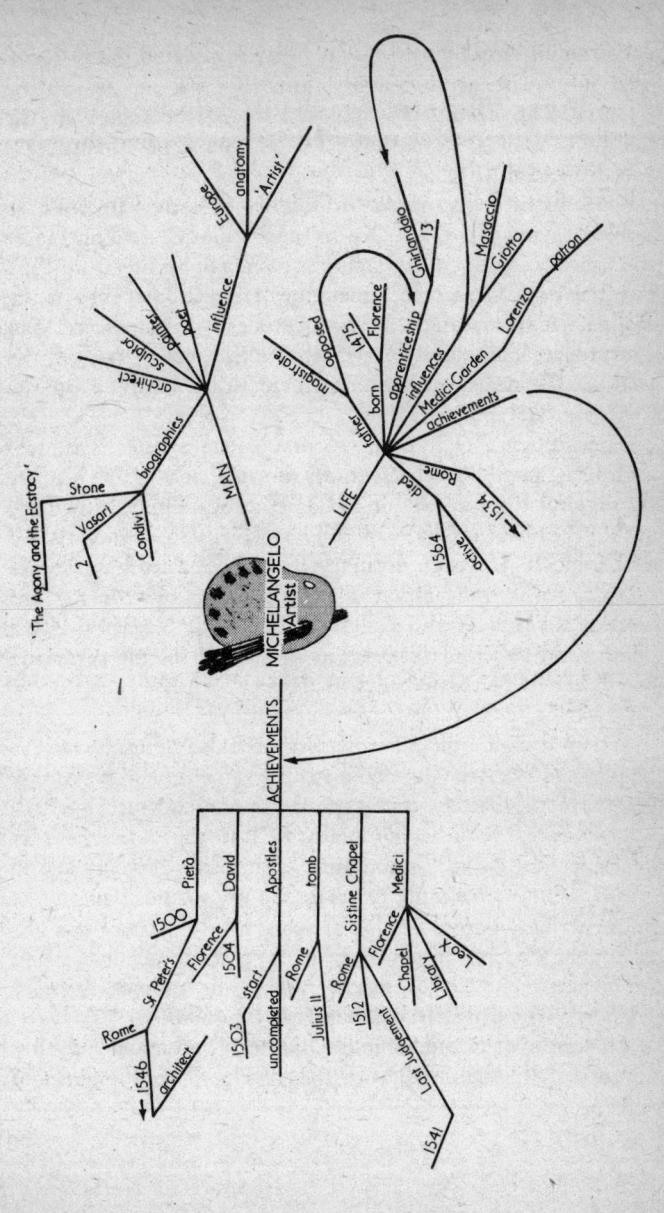

consisted of forty figures. It was never completed in this form. The Pope also commissioned him to work on the Sistine Chapel. The decoration achieved by Michelangelo in the Sistine Chapel is a remarkable feat of art and perseverance. It was finished in 1512.

Once again he returned to Florence, this time to work for Lorenzo's son, Pope Leo X, on the Medici Chapel and later the Library. He spent the last thirty years of his life, from 1534 onwards, in Rome. He added the 'Last Judgement' to the Sistine Chapel, which he completed in 1541. From 1546 onwards he worked as the architect in St Peter's. In 1564, the year of his death, still an active artist, he worked on the *Rondanini Pietà*, now in Milan.

The influence of this remarkable artist (painter, sculptor, architect, poet), was felt both during and after his life throughout Europe. Not only did he innovate by studying the anatomy of the human form, but he also elevated 'the artist' to a position higher than ordinary mortals. Several biographies have been written about him, including two during his lifetime, by Vasari and Condivi, another by Vasari after his death, and a fiction/fact reconstruction of his life by Irving Stone, called *The Agony and the Ecstasy*.

When using a memory pattern to take notes it can be helpful to have two pages going at the same time. On one side you have the pattern form and on the other side you have information that does not really fit into the pattern — for example, formulae quotations, definitions, statistics and graphs. They can simply be related to the various parts of the pattern. The pattern is what you need for review. The accompanying linear notes are likely to contain information which can be more easily learnt by using mnemonics (memory systems), which are discussed later in this chapter.

To review, take the completed pattern and make sure that all the words and images bring the correct information back to mind. The memory pattern is the easiest and most efficient type of note to review. This is because the memory pattern has a unique visual structure which is far easier to commit to memory than page after page of very similar-looking notes. The pattern also shows the connections of the key words in the same order that they tend to be remembered. For these reasons the pattern is more effective to review than a simple list of key words.

You need to commit the structure and the content of the pattern to memory. To do this, you can quickly try to repeat it on another piece of paper. If a piece of the pattern cannot be recalled, check back and make sure that it sticks at the second attempt.

As you review you will find that your memory for patterns automatically improves. Instead of having to write them out or repeat them on a fresh piece of paper you will be able literally to see them in your mind's eye. You can then run through them in your mind's eye and check all the information, making sure that you understand all the key words and that all the key words trigger back the correct information. It is a great advantage when giving a talk or lecture to be able to see the mental image of the pattern and therefore be able to present information with no notes whatsoever.

The whole memory pattern form requires full comprehension when you are making patterns. This means that you have to fully process the information. You can use the pattern form for recalling talks, lectures, television, radio, films, articles, journals, books, meetings, interviews, ideas and plans. The memory pattern can also be used for a diary. As each day is different so is each pattern. You will find that by recording facts, details and names in your diary, you will start to remember automatically much more general information from your everyday life. Your diary then acts as a basic pattern which can be reviewed as necessary. Incidentally, this pattern form can be used for creative as well as recall purposes. If you want to organise your ideas, plan or work on an idea: put the central idea in the middle of the page and then allow your thoughts to well up while quickly jotting them down.

Questions

1 *Surely it is better to have a tidy record of my information in normal linear form?*

Education tends to stress that what is tidy and linear will be memorable. Firstly, you have seen that the best way to remember is to use the key-word form. If you do not use key words there is literally too much information to get through. Also your notes will not be in memory form so that the extra notes interfere with memory. By using the key-word and memory-pattern form you are automatically creating a record which is more natural, more in tune with the way you think. You are also developing a structure of information which shows the inter-linking of one idea with another and represents the whole associative framework of your knowledge. As well as this you are recording a large area of information in a very small area. Whereas before you might have needed ten pages to record the information you wanted, in one pattern you can record the same amount of information, this helping your overall grasp of the information. Everyone, from very young children, school children, university students, through to adults and businessmen finds the pattern form helps their memory and is a highly enjoyable way of recording their ideas and information.

2 *If I have several hundred patterns how do I know when to review a particular pattern?*

This question was partially raised when looking at the review.

It is advisable to set up a review system. One such system is to have a folder with five separate parts. (Each part represents a different review stage.) Each time you complete a pattern you date it. A few minutes after you stop recording information you do review number one. After doing a review you date it with the date of the next review. You then place that pattern into compartment number two, which represents review number two. Every day you quickly look through your whole file. When you come across a piece of paper with today's date on, you then review it. Having reviewed it, you then put the next appropriate review date at the top of the pattern, and replace it in the relevant compartment.

To illustrate this system at work, imagine that on 1 January, you finish a pattern you want to remember, and so you do review number one. Having done the review you then put the appropriate date at the top of the pattern for the next review, which is 2 January. This pattern is then put into compartment number two. When the pattern has worked its way through all five reviews it would look like this:

1 January
2 January
9 January
9 February
9 July

All five reviews should, in total, take no longer than fifteen minutes.

To make sure that you have a well integrated understanding of whatever new information you want to remember it is a good idea to have major memory patterns on the particular subjects or interests you may have. A major memory pattern represents all your knowledge in a particular area. When you construct a new pattern add the new information to your on-going major pattern. This automatically enables you to see how detailed information fits into the overall whole. This is quite often a problem when dealing with large areas of information because it can be difficult to have an overall grasp at the same time as looking at detail. At all times you want not only a microscopic, but also a macroscopic view of your subject or interest.

It is important to note that every time you remember or review information you are not only helping yourself remember that new information but you are also helping yourself remember old information. This is because whenever you remember or learn anything you remember or learn it in relation to what you already know. Therefore, by learning something fresh you can help reinforce the old. In this way your past memories are refreshed every time you take in something new. The more you learn, the more you ensure you can remember what you have already learned!

Living knowledge

What information do you tend to remember most easily? Most people have thousands of images of their personal experience stored in their minds. It is easy for you to remember your real life. Whenever you participate in something, it tends to be more easily remembered than something read or heard. The more active your involvement in anything, the more automatic your memory will be. Again, this is very similar to the idea of processing; it tends not only to be much easier but also more enjoyable to remember an actual experience rather than second-hand experience. Many things are impossible to learn without experience: to learn to fly an aeroplane, to drive a car, to ride a horse, to ride a bicycle, you need the actual experience of doing these things. It is not sufficient just to read and learn about these skills. Similarly, it is much easier for a child to learn and remember any information if he plays an active part in it.

For many people their conventional education offered little

if any of this real experience. However, more recently a trend has developed towards the use of 'living knowledge'. Unfortunately, for many children the classroom conjures up the idea of four bare walls and a teacher pumping in facts which rarely seem to relate to the child's everyday experience. Children are exceptionally good at remembering facts about their own everyday interests (football) and yet they may have incredible difficulty in conventional learning, remembering and taking examinations.

Teachers are trying more and more to encourage children to participate and act out real-life situations. This is particularly the case with very young children who are encouraged to learn by their own experience rather than by being taught. For example, playing with objects is considered an important foundation for the understanding of mathematics in later life. Young children prefer to act out a particular battle strategy rather than having to learn about it from a book. However, as children get older teaching becomes less 'real'. Examinations start to rear their gloomy heads. People have to cram their minds full of facts. And so in many cases there is little time for 'living knowledge'.

Very often, as children begin to find information less relevant, their imagination takes over. They start to daydream: and so pay even less attention. However, this imaginative ability can be well adapted to learning.

The principle of 'living knowledge' is very simple. Whenever you are trying to remember anything, use your imagination to make the information as real and life-like as possible: you can often help do this by imagining *yourself* living out the information to be remembered.

Even in situations where you have no difficulty remembering it is still a good idea to involve your imagination, because this will make your memory even better.

Read the following passage and use your imagination to create mental images.

In the end the Romans left behind them here just three things of value: the first of these would have amused or shocked Caesar, Agricola, and Hadrian for it was Welsh Christianity; the second was the Roman roads; the third, a by-product of the second, was the traditional importance of certain new City sites, especially that of London. But the Latin life of the cities, the villas, the arts, the language and the political organisation of Rome vanished like a dream. The greatest fact in the early history of the island is a negative fact — that the Romans did not succeed in permanently Latinising Britain as they Latinised France.

(*A Shortened History of England*, G. M. Trevelyan)

You may be able to remember that information without making it any more imaginative. However, by injecting imagery into it, you will find that you can remember it more easily and for a much longer time. You might, for example, use the following pictures:

1 Romans leaving Britain — sailing away to France: actually see this picture.
2 Welsh Christianity: imagine a sermon being given by a Welshman, in a broad Welsh accent, and lots of Welshmen (and ladies) in the audience.
3 See a straight Roman road.
4 See city sites, especially an under-developed London.
5 See all Roman influences disappear like ghosts.
6 See Britain as unchanged (no Romans) and France as changed (covered with Romans).

By simply having thought of specific real images to remind yourself of the information you will find that the information will stick. Also, these images will force you to be more attentive when listening as you will continually have to think up appropriate images. Imagination can easily be used to transport yourself back in time and so savour the historical flavour of an era. In so doing, what were previously dry historical facts become exciting 'realities', which do not need *to be* remembered as they *have been* remembered automatically in the same way that a person remembers what he or she did yesterday.

In literature the reader often identifies with and lives through a character in a book. By living through the character, by seeing the world through the character's eyes, the book becomes real and therefore memorable. The author in this case has induced 'living knowledge' by catching the reader's imagination.

Even when information to be remembered does not involve people, the imagination can be harnessed to visualise the facts given. Reading about the universe for example allows the reader to become suspended in space and time as a cosmic observer.

The imagination can be used even further to turn the reader into an inanimate object. In the case, say, of a lecture on economics, you could imagine yourself as a coin or a note inflating and deflating as the various influences on you as a coin or note make themselves felt. You will find that there is no situation where you cannot use your imagination to make the information 'stick'.

If you are trying to grasp the idea of fission (the splitting of the nucleus in the atom — from the Latin *fissio* meaning splitting), you might see yourself as the nucleus splitting into two and so suddenly there becomes two of you. At the same time as you split into two you also let out neutrons (neutral sub-atomic particles) which cause other atoms to split. And so you could see lots of images of yourself being split, setting up a chain reaction. This again will help you remember the idea of fission.

A special application of living knowledge is the use of

drawings when you want to recall a particular idea that can be easily recorded in this permanent form. The drawing below was used in Chapter 1 to illustrate that an animal which receives a blow to the head often loses any memory of what happened immediately prior to the impact.

Memory test

So that you can measure the extent to which the following section will improve your memory performance, try the following test. Read through the list of numbered objects once, trying to remember as much of the whole list — the objects and their correct numbers — as possible. Do not spend more than about thirty seconds on looking at the list. Having looked at the list *do not* write down what you can remember until at least three minutes have passed. During the three-minute period do not mentally run through the list, carry on reading or think about anything except for the list and numbers. The three-minute pause will prevent you from relying on your short-term memory as, for example, you might do in the looking up and dialling of a telephone number.

1 Flame
2 Hand
3 Boat
4 Nut
5 Rain
6 Elephant
7 Dollar
8 Hair
9 Sun
10 Girl

Give yourself a score out of twenty, allowing two marks if you put the right object against the right number. There are no penalty marks. However, you do not score one for simply putting down the number!

Memory systems or Mnemonics (the art of assisting memory; the word is derived from Mnemosyne — the Greek goddess of memory).

The word mnemonics would seem a particularly inappropriate word to describe memory systems, as the word itself is rather difficult to remember in the first place! However, an easy way to remember it is to knock off the M so you leave 'nemonics, and then add an M at the beginning for memory.

Memory systems are simply a way of feeding the memory in a more appropriate manner. They are a way of giving your memory information that is more digestible. In other words, you are applying a new method, or a new means, to assist you to absorb information.

What do you remember best? So far you have seen that you

remember better if you make strong connections and the information is reviewed. You will also know that you tend to remember events that are outstanding. Furthermore, your visual memory tends to be naturally very strong. Memory systems rely upon images that are outstanding. The systems are simply a way of taking advantage of abilities you already have — that is your ability to remember the extraordinary. You probably remember your first car accident, and your first sexual experience, since they are events that have happened to you that were particularly outstanding, and therefore memorable. You also realise that your memory relies very heavily upon association. The idea of association and outstanding images form the basis of mnemonics, which is a simple way of taking advantage of your most natural and effective ways of remembering.

History of mnemonics

These systems were developed by the Greeks. One of the first records of the use of their systems involves Simonides (c 500 BC) who was a Greek poet. He was invited to a large banquet to provide entertainment. After his recitation, Simonides left the banqueting hall which immediately collapsed, killing all the hosts and guests. Simonides was able later to identify the corpses by remembering where each person sat. He linked the seating position with the person who was sitting there. In other words, he linked the place with the person.

This idea of linking some fact or name with a familiar object or place, forms the basis of mnemonics. In this way any list of objects could easily be remembered by linking each object with a specific part of your house and furniture. To recall the objects you simply work your way mentally through the house seeing the objects linked to the predetermined features.

A good memory was of great use to orators and enabled

them to recall the epic stories. These same systems were used by Aristotle, Cicero and St Thomas Acquinas. They were developed through the Middle Ages and today are recognised as a highly effective method of remembering. The systems have been further refined so that they can be used for remembering anything from a telephone number to the cards played in a game of bridge.

It is a good idea to read through the various systems and then to come back and learn the ones best suited for your purposes. The simpler systems are so straightforward that you will be able to remember and apply them immediately.

The Link system

The Link system is one of the most basic methods: say, you wanted to remember the following list:

Apple
Church
Knife
Egg
Lighthouse
Rat
Happy
Ink
Rocket

To remember this list you simply take the first idea and link it with the second. You take the image of the apple and the image of the church and combine them together so as to make a new image. This image must be clearly seen in your mind's eye. The following guidelines will help to make the image outstanding:

1 Keep the image as simple and as straightforward as possible.

2 Exaggerate the sizes of the objects involved. Exaggerated

objects are much easier to remember.

3 If you are remembering an abstract idea, like love, make a solid image — perhaps you might think of two people kissing, or a big heart.

4 Have your images moving wherever possible; things that move are more easily remembered.

5 Make your images colourful and imaginative.

6 Be absurd.

7 Be sexual. (It is amusing to note how the emphasis changes from sexuality to absurdity especially in the over-fifties!)

8 Be humourous.

9 Make use of all the senses. Do not simply see your image: smell it, hear it, feel it, make it as real and lifelike as possible.

Follow these guidelines and simply link your two objects to create a new image. Relax when you are thinking up the images because if you are tense you will find it much harder to conjure them up. You should find that with practice you can think up several such images in a second.

The list you want to remember might be linked in the following way: firstly you have to link *apple* and *church* together — you might see a very large apple walking into a church. As soon as you can see that image put it out of your mind and then move onto the next item on the list.

Your next link is between *church* and *knife* — see yourself in church, the collection bag comes along the row and because you do not have any money on you, you put a large knife into the bag.

You now link *knife* and *egg* — imagine you want to cut a slice of an enormous egg.

The next link is *egg* and *lighthouse* — you might see an egg with a flashing beacon on top.

Lighthouse and *rat* — the lighthouse being beseiged by

monster rats.

Rat and *happy* — (happy is an abstract concept so turn it into a solid image). A child with a massive smile on its face might be a suitable image. So you see a rat performing acrobatics in front of the child as a result of which the child is happy and smiling.

Happy and *ink* — the happy child swimming in a pool of black ink.

Ink and *rocket* — see ink squirting out of the end of the rocket as the method of propulsion.

When creating these images, use your mind as you would a camera, and, having focused on a clear image, take a photograph of it. Once the photograph is taken you need not think any more about the image because if it is sufficiently outstanding you will remember it automatically. You will find that if you lose a particular link it will be for one of these reasons — it was not sufficiently clear, it was too mundane, or it was too complex. Remember that for the purposes of these memory systems you want clear, bizarre and simple images.

Now test yourself with the list of linked images given and see if you can now remember it word for word in the correct order.

Place system

Instead of linking each item with another image, you can link the items to a set series of objects or places familiar to you. This was the system Simonides used when remembering the identity of the guests at the banquet. To use this system you have to first decide on the objects to which you will link whatever it is you want to remember. The objects you choose are your 'pegwords'. The same pegwords can be used over and over again.

As explained earlier, these pegwords could be the main pieces of furniture you see as you walk around your house.

Therefore your pegwords could be:

Stairs
Mirror
Sink
Window
Television
Armchair
    . . . and so on.

When you want to remember a list you simply link the first object to 'stairs' the next to 'mirror', until you have remembered the list. To remember the words, you mentally run through the place pegwords by imagining yourself walking around your house and seeing the links.

Number sound system

This simple system enables you to remember ten objects perfectly in or out of order. The system is based on words which rhyme with the numbers 1–10:

1—Gun
2—Shoe
3—Tree
4—Door
5—Hive
6—Sticks
7—Heaven (make a definite image — see angels and harps or whatever you might hope to find in heaven!)

8—Gate
9—Vine
10—Hen

These rhyming words are pegwords and need to be remembered.

The system can be applied to the memory test at the beginning of this section.

Number 1 is gun; number 1 in the original test was *flame*. So you need to link gun and flame, to produce a new image.

You can use this system all the time, to remember what you want to do during the day, or simply to remember the items

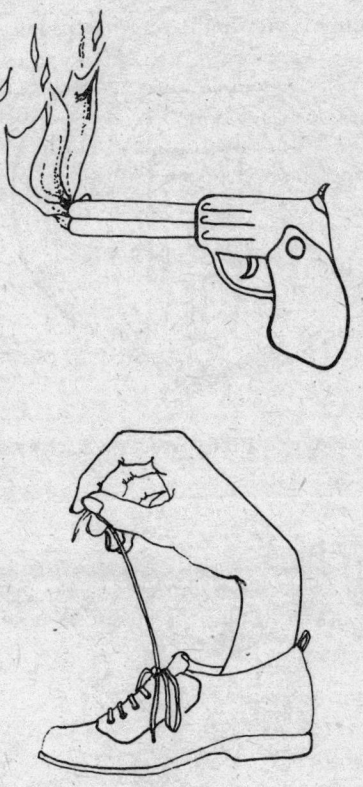

2 is shoe: you want to remember *hand*.

3 is tree: you want to remember *boat*.

4 is door: you want to associate it with *nut*.

5 is hive: you want to link this with *rain*.

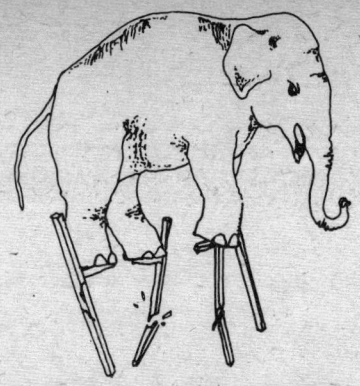

6 is sticks and you want to associate this with *elephant*.

7 is heaven: you want to remember *dollar*.

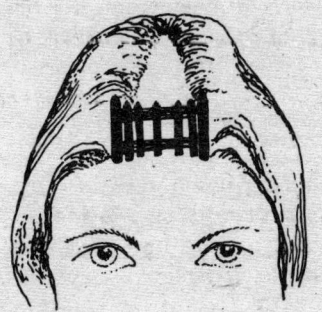

8 is gate: you want to associate this with *hair*.

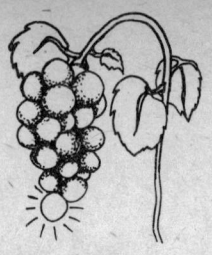

9 is vine and you want to remember *sun*.

10 is hen: you want to remember *girl*.

on your shopping list. Rather than jotting these things down, when you want to remember them, use these systems. By doing this you will find that you really will be able to rely on your memory.

Number-shape system

Similar to the number-sound system is the number-shape system, but instead of utilising words that sound like the particular numbers, you substitute objects that look like the numbers. For example, you might use the following shapes for the numbers:

1—Telegraph pole
2—Swan
3—Buttocks, or the end of a bone
4—The sail of a boat
5—Half a cherry, or a scythe
6—A snake
7—A cliff
8—An hour glass
9—A golf club, or flag pole
10—A bouncing ball

The method of using this system is exactly the same as the number sound system, except that the pegwords are different.

Alphabet system
This system uses the letters of the alphabet instead of numbers, instead of having one = gun, here you have a list of words each starting with the sound of the appropriate letter:

a—Ace	b—Bee	c—Sea
d—Deed	e—Easel	f—Effigy
g—Jeep	h—H-bomb	i—Eye
j—Jay	k—Cage	l—Elastic
m—Ember	n—Enamel	o—Oboe
p—Pea	q—Queue	r—Artist
s—Eskimo	t—Tea	u—U-boat
v—Vehicle	w—W-C	x—X-ray
y—Wife	z—Zebra	

The system enables you to remember twenty-six objects perfectly in or out of alphabetical order, using the same imaginative links between the pegwords and the items you want to remember. The alphabet system can also be used to remember letter combinations. If you wanted to remember the letters THSA, using the alphabet system, you need to link T, which is tea, to H, which is H-bomb. For this you could imagine pouring some tea onto an H-bomb. Then you link H-bomb to S, which is eskimo. Here you could imagine an H-bomb being eaten by a hungry eskimo. Then you have to link eskimo to A, which is ace. For this you could imagine an eskimo playing with a pack of cards which is so large that he can hardly pick up the ace.

These four basic methods, the Link method, the number-sound method, the number-shape system and the Alphabet system are all very easy to learn and of immediate practical use. It is important to start applying them immediately and to get into the habit of using them.

Questions

1 *Surely, once I have used a particular system, for example, the number-sound system, I cannot use that system again since the old images will be confused with the new images?*
You can use the same system over and over again. Indeed, you can use one system several times a day.

The words in the number-sound system: gun, shoe, tree, door, hive, etc; and in the alphabet system: ace, bee, sea, etc, are the pegwords for linking your new information. These pegwords are rather like the pegs in a cloakroom which can be used time and time again. Although you may be able to remember the older images, you will find that the most recent images are the first to be recalled. To avoid any possibility of interference between the images, however, it is advisable to use each system only once a day, and therefore it is useful to master more than one of these systems.

2 *Isn't this all a rather complicated method of doing something which should be simple?*
These systems are of great use with the type of information which is not easily reviewed and not easily memorised. The sort of information you very often have difficulty with, like

disconnected events, facts and everyday lists. Mastering a system takes a very short time. Their application is immediate. Furthermore, actually using the system is fun. You find that whereas before you had to write down a simple list of facts, you can now commit them to memory in less time than it would have taken to write them down!

3 *Although I can see that the systems are very effective for remembering lists and such like — are there any more advanced systems for remembering a very long series of facts or figures that perhaps I want to commit to memory for a very long time?*

There are several systems of a more advanced nature, one of the most useful of these is the number letter or 'T for one' system.

'T for one' system

Firstly you must spend a short time mastering the basic table below. As you can see the numbers from zero to 9 are represented by a letter (or letters) from the alphabet.

1 — T or D
2 — N
3 — M
4 — R
5 — L
6 — CH, SH, or J
7 — K, hard G or C
8 — F or V
9 — P or B
0 — S or Z

These letters can combine to represent any number between one and a thousand. To create a pegword take the appropriate letters for the number and turn them into a word. Ensure that you use only 'neutral' letters with the number letters. The numbers 1–20 and 20, 30 etc, to 100 can be represented as follows;

1 — Tie or Tea	10 — Toes	20 — Nose
2 — Noah	11 — Tate	30 — Mice
3 — Ma	12 — Tan or Tin or Dune	40 — Rose
4 — Ray or Rye	13 — Dime or Tome	50 — Lace
5 — Law	14 — Tar or Tyre	60 — Chase or Cheese
6 — Shoe or Jaw	15 — Tail	70 — Case
7 — Key or Cow	16 — Dish or Taj (Mahal)	80 — Face
8 — Foe	17 — Tack	90 — Base or Bus
9 — Pa or Bee	18 — Toffee	100 — Disease
	19 — Tap or Tub	

Having mastered the basic code you can immediately use this 'T for one' system to remember a hundred objects. You can also use it to convert numbers into images and so remember number sequences like telephone numbers. If you wanted to remember the telephone number 460 9510, you would first convert it into words: riches (460), ball (95), toes (10). To remember the particular sequence you link the image of riches to ball to toes. Therefore, you might imagine millions of pound notes wrapped to make a massive ball which bounces onto your toes. You will usually want to remember whose telephone number it is that you are remembering; in which case link either the first or the last image to the person concerned. So either you could imagine the person with all the notes or you could imagine the ball bouncing on their toes.

You can use this system to remember dates and facts as well. For example, if you want to remember that the atomic bomb was dropped on Hiroshima in 1945, 1945 converts into (19 = tap) and (45 = rail). To make the link you might see a sequence of images like this: a very large tap being blown into the air and landing several miles away on a railway track.

You might want to remember that the effective beginning of the Russian Empire was in 1721. Here 1721 converts into tack (17), net (21). And so you want to link Russia — tack net.

Having completed a series of images always make sure that you can quickly repeat the words in sequence, and make sure that the images are as simple as possible and that exactly the correct information is recalled.

Questions

4 *Surely if I am not sufficiently interested in something to remember it automatically I should not bother to try and remember it at all?*
I agree that it would be better if all learning was so interesting that the process required no special effort; however, there is much information which is difficult to remember and in the long term you can save yourself a lot of time by remembering certain facts. Using a system for this type of learning is far less of a strain than sitting down and trying to repeat a fact over and over again, occasionally pulling out your hair in despair when you find that you have just forgotten something that you committed to memory a few minutes before!

Names

5 *Is there any way I can adapt these memory systems to help my memory for names and faces?*
By using the basic idea of association you can make sure that you always have a good memory for names and faces. When trying to remember a name you need to link that particular name to the face of the person. Firstly, when you are introduced to someone make sure that you hear the name. If it is a complicated or foreign name you can ask for the name to be repeated and if necessary spelt. Remain relaxed, or otherwise you may not even hear the name. As soon as you have clearly registered the name try to use it. For example,

having been introduced to a Mrs Long, use her name when talking back to her. The Americans have developed a reputation for over-using this technique. An American having been introduced to a person called George may thereafter not stop repeating his name and so say, 'Well, George, what do you think about . . .? Really George? — Hey, everybody listen to this, George thinks that . . . Don't you George? . . . George, you really are some guy — yes, George, you really are, George!' This sort of over-use will probably put off the average Englishman, particularly since he has almost certainly forgotten the other's name!

Having made sure you heard the name, repeat it. The next thing you need to do is to link the name of that person with a prominent feature of his or her face. Select the feature you think is most prominent, and exaggerate it in your mind's eye: then link the chosen feature to the name in some image form. The easiest way to explain this is to give a series of examples. If I meet Mr Warren I look for his main feature. Mr Warren has a very large nose — and so I create an image of rabbits hopping in and out of his nose.

If Mr Robinson has large blue eyes you might imagine his eyes squinting in the bright sun looking over the sea from a desert island (Robinson Crusoe).

If Mr Russell has large earlobes, imagine them flapping in the wind like leaves on a tree and hear them go 'rustle', 'rustle', 'rustle'.

Christian names can be remembered by choosing a word that sounds like the Christian name: Harry can become hairy; James — dames; Robert — robber. In other words, you set up your own code system and link a particular feature of the face with the Christian-name substitute. Once you decide on a code, stay with the same words. If you meet somebody called James who has big lips you might see a row of dames sitting on the lower lip. If Harry has very fat cheeks you might imagine that he has a mouthful of hair.

Another method of remembering Christian names is to simply link a feature from the face of the person you have been introduced to, to a person you already know with the same name. So you have just met Richard, who has long sideboards: link him to your own friend Richard by picturing his swinging on these sideboards.

It can be particularly difficult to link a name to a facial feature if the name is very unfamiliar. Whenever you come across a name or a piece of information that is unfamiliar you want to try to make it more familiar. A way to do this is to say the name over to yourself time and time (and time) again; you will usually find that the name will break down into constituent parts that you can recognise. If you were introduced to a Mr Leonidas: how could you make certain you remembered that name? Firstly, you say the name over to yourself several times. Then you decide what the name reminds you of: what the name sounds like. What words can you find that make up the name? In this case you might think of the words lion and Daz (the washing powder) so the image you create here might be that of a lion washing in Daz.

It would be particularly easy to remember the name 'Mr Leonidas' if Mr Leonidas has very long blond hair! Do try, when you are dealing with unfamiliar information to think about it, in this way the unfamiliar will soon become familiar.

6 Do I need to use these memory systems all the time?
Mnemonics are a way of sharpening your memory and keeping it fit. The success of these methods gives you confidence immediately. In the long term you will find that your memory improves to such an extent that only rarely will you need to use the systems.

Vocabulary

Learning new vocabulary, either of your own language or of

another language, is difficult because the words tend to be unfamiliar. There are two ways you can help your memory for words generally. Firstly, whenever you are looking up a word in a dictionary have a look at its derivation — a knowledge of Greek or Latin can be a great help here. The second method of assisting your memory for words is to convert them into more familiar, understandable words. Use the technique already described for remembering names, say the word over to yourself several times. Having done that you will probably find that the new word reminds you of a word or a series of words you already know. For example, if you were trying to remember the word, Marsala (a sweet white wine). The first thing to do is to say the word over to yourself until it reminds you of a word or words you already know. This word can be broken down into 'ma' 'cellar'. By saying these two words you will be reminded of the word, Marsala. Very quickly you will find that you remember the word automatically.

To remember the meaning of the word you need to associate 'ma' and 'cellar' with a wine. To do this you might imagine your ma, sitting in the cellar drunk because she has had too much white wine.

A slightly more complex example is the word, tautology. (A tautology means expressing the same thing twice in different words — eg, . . . arrived one after the other in succession). Saying the word tautology over to yourself a few times, it can be broken down into: taut, toll, orgy. And so to help remember the word itself think of a very *taut toll* (bridge) on which there is an *orgy*. To help yourself with the meaning it would be a good idea to remember the example given above. You could imagine that you are standing on a taut toll (bridge) in a queue, having arrived one after the other in succession, to join the orgy!

Onomatopeia means a word which sounds like the thing it describes, like cuckoo or the buzz of a bee. The word can be broken down into: on, mat, pee, which should be enough to remind you of the word onomatopeia. It requires little imagination to construct an image which will recall the word and the meaning. Often it is only necessary to use part of a word to bring back the whole word.

The vocabulary of foreign languages is just as easy to remember, using the same technique. The Spanish for a puddle is '*charco*'. The word '*charco*' perhaps reminds you of the word charcoal. In this case you could imagine putting a large piece of burning charcoal in a puddle.

The German for station is '*der Bahnhof*'. You could imagine a barn with trains inside. 'Skirt' is '*der Rock*' and so you could imagine a woman trying on a rock instead of a skirt. Through these images you remember the word and the meaning.

Be careful to avoid creating images that are too ordinary. You might, for example, when applying this system to the French word '*la maison*' (house), picture a stone mason building a house. This image would not be extraordinary or outstanding and therefore not particularly memorable.

All these memory links need only be used to begin with, since very quickly the memory will become automatic. However, if you do not use a system to begin with you actually waste time. Children taught foreign vocabulary using this type of method will usually perform several times better than children taught by other rote methods.

Speeches and talks

When you are giving a talk, speech or lecture, there are two reliable methods for assisting your memory. Firstly, you can talk from a memory pattern. Providing the memory pattern has been fully reviewed, you will be able to see it clearly in your mind's eye. If you prefer, you can have the pattern in front of you and refer to it as necessary. Alternatively, a memory system is a great help. Once you have worked out your speech and decided the order of what you want to say, select the main key words that represent the sections of the speech. You then use the link system or the number-sound system, or the number-shape system, the alphabet system or the 'T for one' system to remember the key words in order. During your talk you simply run through your memorised key words. One fear which people sometimes have is that they will suddenly have a complete mental blank. To some extent you can be sure that you will not run this risk if you are talking from a well reviewed pattern or well rehearsed memory system. However, to overcome the fear you can reassure yourself by having a list of the key words nearby, so that you can quickly refer to the list if need be. You will find that by having this reassuring prop you do not forget anyway and so subsequently gain sufficient confidence to work without any notes.

Dreams

Some people believe that they do not dream at all! Others say that they always dream. In fact, everyone dreams when they are asleep. If you think that you do not dream very much, you probably have noticed that you tend to dream more when you have a bad night's sleep. When you have indigestion, are ill, or in a strange and uncomfortable bed, you will find that you tend to remember more of your dreams than you do normally. The word remember is important here because all that happens is that you sleep less heavily and therefore think about and remember more dreams.

Whenever you want to help yourself to recall your dreams, the first thing is to pre-set yourself to remember. If I ask a group of people just how many of them had dreams the night before, perhaps less than a third of the group will say that they did dream. However, when I tell them that I want them all to come back the next day with at least two or three dreams, nearly all of them will remember at least one dream. The best way to pre-set yourself to do this is to remind yourself, before you go to sleep, that you are going to remember your dreams.

Many people who remember dreams when they first wake up, forget them shortly afterwards. To hold the memory of a dream you need to make some form of record of the dream immediately. Leave a notepad and pencil by the bedside and whenever you wake up and can remember a dream write it down. Alternatively you can use a memory system to remember the key events of the dream (you might use the number-sound or number-shape system). Make sure that you remain relaxed while you are linking the dream event to your peg word, otherwise your dream may disappear. If you use a mnemonic system it is a good idea to write the dream down later on during the day.

Immediate recall during examinations

All the memory systems give you immediate recall. You can use the 'T for one' system to remember a thousand facts for life. When taking examinations, you want to use both mnemonics and the pattern form.

The best method of approaching an examination paper is, having thoroughly read through the instructions and examination questions, firstly, to select the questions you wish to answer, and then to decide how much time you can allow for each question. However, do not start writing until you have first put down on a piece of paper the relevant memory pattern and/or mnemonic. Before writing the answer to your first question jot down the pattern and memory system for the *second* question that you have decided to answer. In other words, you always want to prepare one question ahead of the question you are answering. By doing this you will find that your memory gets to work on the next question while you are writing the first answer and you will come up with new ideas and information during the examination rather than after it.

Reminders, times and dates

A very useful system for remembering to carry out certain tasks is the place association method. This simply means that you associate what you need to remember to do with an object you are bound to come across during the day. To help you remember to go to the chemist, you could link your front door with a large medicine bottle and so imagine a bottle instead of the door. Providing you see this image clearly you will find that on leaving the house and seeing the front door you will automatically remember that you need to go to the chemist.

You can use this method to remember anything during the day and so avoid absentmindedness. Link what you need to do, link what you need to remember, with an object you are certain to see. This method can also be used to remind you of what you want to say to a particular person. If you want to remember to ask a friend where you could buy a good pair of shoes, you could help yourself remember to do this by seeing your friend in a massive pair of boots — a pair of boots so large that you can only just see the top of his head. Again, you will find that when you meet this person you will automatically remember the image and so remember to ask the question.

Times, dates and appointments can easily be converted into the 'T for one' system. For a dentist appointment at 12 o'clock you could imagine your dentist standing on a dune (12 in the 'T for one' system) in the desert, waving his drill at you. Use the 24-hour clock if you have appointments which could be either day or night. Obviously it is pretty unlikely that you will need to go and see your dentist at midnight! If you do not want to use the 24-hour clock you can simply place your images either in daylight to represent am or in candlelight to represent pm.

Your schedule for a whole week can be remembered by representing the days of the week, that is Sunday right through to Saturday, as the numbers one to seven. If you have an appointment with your dentist on Tuesday (the third day of the week), at 10 o'clock, that equals 310. 310 in the 'T for one' system converts into *maids*. You might see your dentist surrounded by hundreds of beautiful maids.

Use the same method for remembering dates and especially birthdays. 18 December, for example, converts as 18 — toffee, 12 — tan. In this case you could see the person whose birthday it is eating a huge bar of melting toffee while he or she is getting tanned in the sun.

The senses

When you are using these memory systems try to use more than one sense. Try to experience what you are imagining through all the senses. When you were trying to remember the birthday on 18 December, you created a series of images. To make them really memorable, it is not enough to just see the images, you should capture the smell, the taste, the stickiness and the heat; bring as many senses as possible to bear on the images.

Sometimes one sense will automatically trigger off another sense. Listening to music may make you feel either warm or cold; some people see music in colours. This ability to use several senses together is called synaesthesia. It is an ability which everyone possesses to some extent, and can certainly be developed. When you see a picture of a stormy sea, you may suddenly feel the wind against your face, the salt drying on your lips and hear the lashing waves and the buffeting sea. This is what is meant by using as many senses as possible. By using extra senses you are automatically making new relationships and therefore more connections.

101

To help yourself develop this extra sense of awareness use a sense other than vision in the memory training. When you use the number-sound system — instead of seeing a picture of the image — try feeling the object or smelling it, or listening to it, or touching it. Then take that sense image and link it with what you want to remember. If you needed to link 1 (in number sound — gun), with tar and you have decided to use your sense of touch, firstly, you would feel the gun to find out what it is like to touch and then imagine yourself feeling tar, feeling its stickiness, feeling the way it clings to your hand. Then blend those two sensations and create a new sensation by combining the metallic touch of the gun with the stickiness of the tar. Through using your other senses you will give yourself five times the number of memory systems that you already have.

You can be even more adventurous and combine different senses. In the above example you might remember gun through the sound and tar through the smell. You hear the 'bang' of the gun and you need to link this to the strong stench of the tar. This sort of exercise will immediately help you to develop your memory of senses generally.

Card memory system

The 'T for one' system can also be applied in the memorising of a pack of cards. The actual feat of remembering a sequence of cards in or out of order is very impressive. However, it has great practical advantages if you are a card player, especially in the games which require a good memory of those cards which have already been dealt or played. To remember fifty-two cards in or out of sequence you need to remember perfectly 1 – 52 in the 'T for one' series. The numbers 1 – 20 have already been given. Suggestions for the numbers 20 – 52 are given at the top of the opposite page.

20—Nose	31—Mat	42—Run
21—Net	32—Man	43—Ram
22—Nun	33—Mama	44—Rear
23—Name	34—Mare	45—Rail
24—Nero	35—Male	46—Rash
25—Nail	36—Mash	47—Rack
26—Niche	37—Mac	48—RAF or Rave
27—Neck	38—Mafia	49—Rape
28—Nave	39—Map	50—Lace
29—Nap	40—Rose	51—Lad
30—Mice	41—Rat	52—Lane

An individual image must be created for each card in the pack. To do this you take the first letter of each suit: spades (s), diamonds (d), hearts (h), clubs (c). Each card also takes on the appropriate letter from the 'T for one' series. Therefore, the two of spades is going to begin with 's' and end in 'n', making the word 'sun'. Count the aces as one.

	Spades	Diamonds	Hearts	Clubs
Ace (1)	Soot	Dot	Hat	Cat
2	Sun	Dune	Hen	Can
3	Sum	Dame	Ham	Comb
4	Sore	Deer	Hair	Car
5	Sail	Doll	Hail	Coal
6	Sash	Dish	Hash	Cash
7	Sack	Duck	Hiccup	Cake
8	Safe	Dove	Hive	Cave
9	Sap	Dip	Hip	Cap
10	Squeeze	Dice	Hose	Case

To remember the jacks of each suit, simply see a picture of whatever suit they stand for. Therefore, for the jack of spades, simply see a spade, the jack of diamonds see a diamond, etc. The queens and kings can be equally easily learnt by associating the queen or the king with their appropriate suit. For example, for the queen of spades you simply see a lady digging, for the queen of diamonds you see a woman holding a very large diamond; for the queen of hearts you see the queen holding her broken heart. For the queen of clubs you see a woman perhaps playing golf. For the king of spades you see an old king resting on his spade, for the king of diamonds you see an old man wearing a crown of huge diamonds, for the king of hearts you see a man holding his failing heart and finally, for the king of clubs, you see a king whirling a club. Using the 'T for one' system in conjunction with this adaptation of that system you can remember any sequence of cards in order. You can also remember what cards have gone during a game.

There are some card games in which it is necessary to know which cards have not gone, rather than those that have. In this case, every time a card is played you simply destroy the image of that card in your mind. For example, if somebody plays the three of diamonds, you take the word-picture for that card, in this case 'dame', and destroy it — by burning it, drowning it, or however you like. As you quickly run through the cards, the undestroyed images will represent the cards that have not yet been played.

Over the last few years, these memory systems have had an exciting reappraisal. Much research work is being undertaken on the systems and the reasons for their success. They are already being used extensively in language teaching and in specialised fields, such as the helping and curing of verbal defects. The systems are so successful that researchers are beginning to say that they are among the most potent memory factors ever discovered. So for your own development it is important to grasp the basic principles of association. It is a good idea to learn the basic systems and best of all learn the longer 'T for one' system. If you tried the test at the beginning of this section now re-take the test at the end. You will not only find that you can do this test with much greater ease, you will recognise that you could do a test anything up to ten times this length!

Second memory test

Use one of the systems to remember the following list. Spend no more than about thirty seconds on the list and then wait three minutes before writing out the list, perfectly!

1 Child
2 Dog
3 Table
4 Car
5 Stair
6 Train
7 Sea
8 Glass
9 Coal
10 Squirrel

As in the test at the beginning of the chapter, mark yourself out of twenty. You will find that you have scored much better than in the original test — you should have scored 100 per cent. A 100 per cent score is what you should always aim for with these mnemonics. This simple 1 – 10 list should now be an exceptionally straightforward task.

Summary

X 'Memory Patterns'. Use key words and images to record links between facts and ideas in a visually different and unique way

X To review a pattern make sure all the information required is triggered back by the pattern and that you can fully repeat the structure and content of the pattern

X Living knowledge uses the imagination to enrich and make real all information.

X Memory systems, originally developed by the Greeks, rely on the association of outstanding images, naturally a good way to remember

X The systems usually have special pegwords that are linked with the fact or object to be remembered

X The images want to be as outstanding as possible and this can be helped by being humourous, colourful, sensual, imaginative in the linking of the images. Names can be easily remembered by linking the name with a prominent feature of the face

X Vocabulary is quickly learnt by linking the image of a familiar word with the meaning of a new word. Speeches and talks can be remembered by having a well reviewed pattern or by using a memory system. The systems can be further used to remember appointments, dates, dreams and playing cards

X By combining the five senses you increase the strength of the images in the systems. You can also use one sense for the pegwords and another for the objects to be remembered

4 Effects of Memory on Performance and Outlook

Information set — Types of memory set: negative and positive — Negative language, suggestion, thinking, and pessimistic outlook — Objective analysis — Imagery — Unproductive use of memory — Static memory, static words and ideas

In previous chapters you have seen how memory directly affects interest. The greater the body of knowledge (memory) the greater tends to be the number of possible connections, and the greater the interest. Knowledge therefore helps and encourages you to remember new information. In this way your memory gives your mind a particular direction, an outlook, a definite 'set'. Your mind tends to be set towards areas in which you already have information and experience.

A designer of clothes or cars will quickly notice a new fashion or style. Equally, a landscape gardener will notice much more of a garden than a casual visitor.

Information set

Whenever you are set for information you actually notice it with greater ease and speed than if you are not set.

This can be illustrated by the following experiment: you are looking at a screen onto which is flashed, one at a time, and at random, each letter of the alphabet. It will take you almost exactly the same time to recognise each letter. However, if instead of expecting a random letter of the alphabet, you are told that only the letter 'A' or the letter 'B' is to be flashed onto the screen, you will recognise the letter more quickly. Therefore, in the pre-set condition your recognition is speeded up. Conversely, when pre-set it can be particularly difficult to recognise something that you are not expecting. An example of this is where you meet a person whom you know, in a strange setting. Because the setting is different to the one in which you would normally meet that person you are not 'set' to meet that person. You may, therefore, find it difficult to remember his name. There are many situations where people generally pre-set themselves — when people come across a foreigner they are very fast to recognise certain national characteristics that they expect to recognise; if you are particularly frightened you will tend to interpret everything going on around you in a particularly frightening way; if you decide that a particular day is exceptionally depressing you will be set to see information that confirms the fact that the day is depressing.

Magicians rely to a large extent on pre-setting their audience to see and believe what they want them to see and believe. In this way the audience will not usually notice the obvious trick involved in the 'magic'. These are all examples of short-term set, and are the sort of sets which may affect you for a few minutes or perhaps hours. However, many of the short-term sets blend into a much longer-term set. A long-term set reveals itself in people's biases, opinions, leanings, dispositions, bigotry, prejudice and interests.

To illustrate the different ways in which people can be set, imagine two people, James and Helen, who go for a walk in a forest. James is particularly interested in trees, in fact he is a naturalist. Helen finds the forest oppressive and has no interest in nature. Helen is agitated and nervous. She is frightened because she associates trees with danger.

James is oblivious to any danger because he is so interested in his surroundings. He is observing and learning all the time. Helen's imagination is running wild. (It is an interesting fact

108

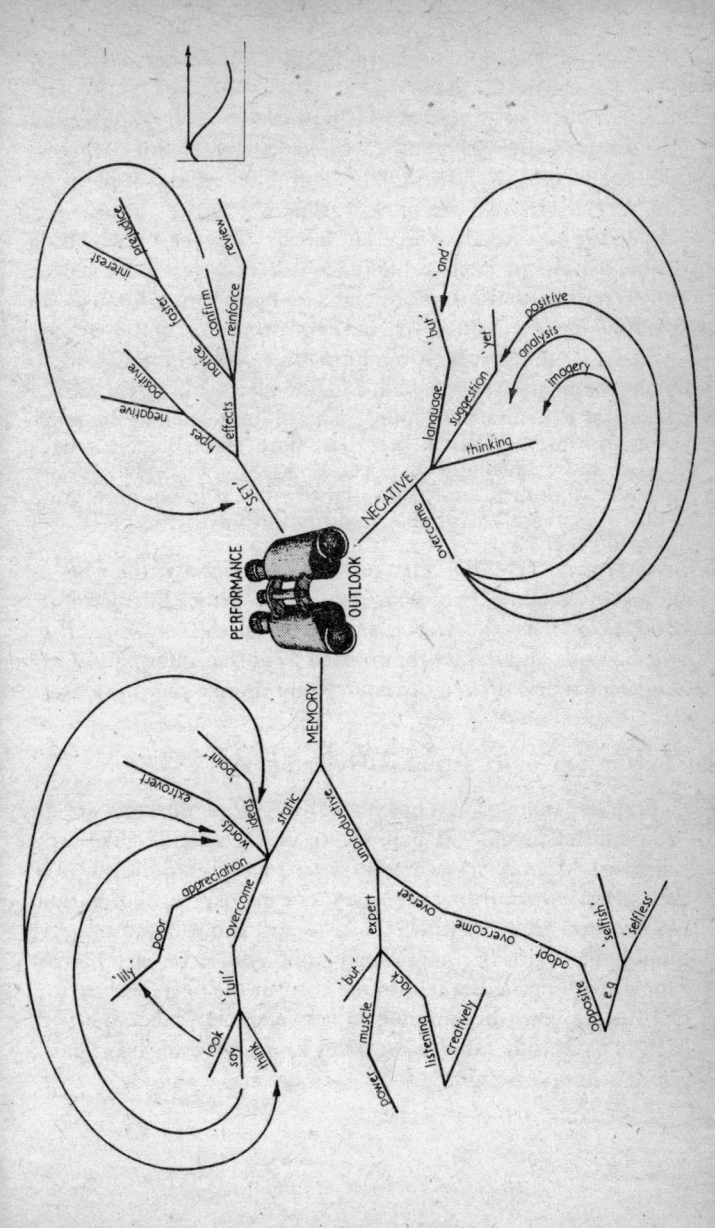

that very often people's creative imagination works most when they are fearing imminent disaster!)

Why is it that James and Helen experience and appreciate the forest in such different ways? The forest, that is the trees, the undergrowth, the smell, and the whole feeling, is interpreted in two completely different ways. James and Helen are experiencing different forests! The reason why they are experiencing such a difference is because they are set for different information. Their set has been 'programmed' by past information and experience, and as a result of the set they will notice things which reinforce that programming and so make that experience and information all the more real.

This is the same principle as is used in reviewing. By going over the information it becomes more available for recall. Being more available for recall it is then more easily associated, linked and connected to what is going on around you. This readily available information forms the basis of a person's mental set.

You see, therefore, that no two people's idea of what is going on around them will ever be the same. Furthermore, how people see the world is reflected in the information in their minds and the set that results from that information. By adopting a new set you can completely change your outlook.

Types of memory set: negative and positive

There are many different types of set. Your interests are an example of mental set and so are your particular likes and dislikes. Mental set is a term which simply applies to how prepared you are for a particular category of information. Where you are set to tune in to a subject, you will notice it that much more easily. Let us say that you have just bought something, perhaps a pair of shoes — for the next few hours or even days you will continue to notice similar shoes. You are set, that is your mind is working in the general direction to notice that type of shoe.

The same effect is noticeable when you come across an unfamiliar word in a book. Whether or not you look up that word in a dictionary, you seem to keep coming across it with uncanny regularity. You are not, in fact, coming across the word any more often, but are set to notice it because it has been particularly brought to your attention.

Two general sets often referred to are the negative and the positive set. This general distinction has given rise to much of the writing on positive and negative thinking. A negative set will be more inclined to stress the negative aspects of any situation. A very negative set might involve the following beliefs:

1 That a third world war was imminent.
2 That world-wide famine could not be checked.
3 That human nature was such that it was not really worth bothering about either of the above anyway!

On the other hand a positive set, although it might recognise such possible dangers, would be more inclined to look for ways to avert such disaster.

What is the effect of a very negative set? Firstly, because you are reviewing predominantly negative information it will make it all the more available for recall. Because the information is easily available for recall this will encourage you to have a negative set. You will therefore be more inclined to notice negative information to support your general negative set.

Everyone likes to have their opinions confirmed; this all ties in with what was referred to as your self-proving ability. With negative information, and a negative set, you will tend to prove both the set and the information. Worst of all, you will perhaps act in accordance with your negative beliefs. If enough people act in accordance with those negative beliefs, what was originally just a negative interpretation could actually become reality! In other words, if enough people believed that a world war is imminent, that famine is round

111

the corner and that human nature is not worth bothering about, the chances are that these conditions will actually develop. On the other hand, people with a positive set will be far more willing and able to change the situation. A positive set makes a person more confident about achievement and success. Confidence automatically plays an important role in any change. Without confidence people rarely start to do anything.

A person with a negative set behaves rather like a faulty tape recorder which is only picking up certain frequencies. This tape recorder might hear a symphony as one or two discordant notes, and the coughing and shuffling of the audience. The positive set is rather like a tape recorder which catches the full effect and impact of the symphony. Subsequently, when either of these tapes are played back they will reinforce the original impression. The negative tape becomes even more negative and the positive tape becomes even more positive.

A person with a generally negative set will very often make negative links and connections. Even new information will be added to the growing negative store of experience, and the more this is done, the easier it becomes to interpret everything in a negative way. This type of negative set grows like a cancer until only the negative aspects of a situation are recognisable. The tape recorder only has a record of a minute area of information which is all of one particular type. Furthermore, all this information confirms existing beliefs. The person, therefore, believes he is right.

Two spectators at a football match may see a completely different game because of their set. For one the day was cold, his feet frozen, the football — if it could be described as such — was atrocious and the team he supported only won by three goals. The other found he was a little hoarse, exhausted from the excitement and thrilled by the show of expert professional football. He hardly noticed that his team had lost.

112

You may think that difference is a question of personalities. Partially perhaps, but what you notice outside you is usually a reflection of what you are thinking, remembering and reviewing inside. It is hardly surprising that, after many years of negative playback a person can have such a negative outlook as to be totally blind to any positive characteristics whatsoever!

You notice and remember things similar to your own thoughts. Furthermore, people with similar outlooks and memories come together and so further confirm a positive or negative approach. Therefore there are distinct groups — the foretellers of doom and disaster, and the believers in the potential of mankind. Neither can be absolutely right or wrong, however, I prefer to be a member of the second group because they tend to be constructive rather than destructive!

The next section of this chapter will look at the symptoms of negative set, and will help you to watch for it in yourself and in other people.

Negative language and suggestion

You use words to communicate ideas and meaning to yourself and other people. Some words, however, begin to affect the actual ideas you have. The classic example of this is the person who uses the word 'but'. This word tends to encourage negative comment. When you use 'but' you will often rely upon negative information to back up that 'but'. This means you will keep playing over negative information which reinforces it as you review it. The more often you review it the easier it is to remember and, therefore, use again. Examples of 'but' include: 'that's a good idea, *but*', 'I would like to, *but*', 'It is really very simple, *but*'. You sometimes hear a person 'but'ing — that is, he keeps trying to interrupt what you are saying with a 'but'. When this word is used it generally detracts from what is being said or suggested rather than continuing or developing what is being said.

Instead of saying, 'That is a good idea, *but*', you can say, 'That is a good idea *and* I think it would be very useful if we stressed etc . . .' This use of 'and' encourages more constructive comment, and compliments rather than puts down the person talking. Next time you are in conversation and you feel like contradicting or disagreeing, try and use the word 'and', and you will normally find that your comments become far more productive. You will be more inclined to produce productive and positive ideas which, because they have been reviewed, will be more available in the future. 'But' is a word which can be used positively, however it tends to encourage negative and unproductive playback of your memories.

There are other words and phrases which also encourage negative recall, like '*can't*', '*don't*', '*would not*'. When you say, 'I cannot come to see you tomorrow because I must do . . . etc', by using the word 'cannot' you are encouraged to find reasons why not. Instead you might try saying, 'I have a lot to do tomorrow and so because I am coming to see you tomorrow I must do . . .'. By simply revising the sentence, removing a 'cannot' or 'don't', you find you start thinking in a more positive, more active way.

You may say, well what has all this to do with memory? Words like 'not' and 'but' are trigger words which encourage constant recall of negative or unproductive ideas in your memory. The more negative your outlook becomes the harder it is to make any positive connection.

Similar to negative language is negative suggestion. In everyday conversation it is easy to plant negative emphasis. The negative emphasis will again give the mind a set. This set will tend to find information. The information confirms the set. And so you believe that your suggestion is right.

A child's education can be hindered by negative suggestions. By suggesting, by planting the idea in a child's mind that he is not necessarily good at a particular subject, he will often fail to do well in that subject. Accordingly the child begins to prove that belief in his performance, and the negative suggestion becomes a reality. When you come across someone who talks and thinks negatively, be careful how you point this out, because the person planting these negative time bombs is likely to blow up in your face!

If you are asked the question, 'Have you had flu yet this year?', or, 'Have you had a car accident yet?', both these questions can easily be answered with a simple 'yes' or 'no'. However, looking more closely at the sentence, what do you notice? There is the implication through the use of the word *yet* that there is the probability if not the certainty that you are going to have flu or an accident. You therefore begin to think that it is quite normal to expect to have flu or an accident. You really ought to question the question. Is there any reason why you should have flu or an accident?

Whereas a negative suggestion is powerful and destructive, positive suggestion is equally powerful and far more productive. The French psychologist, Emile Coué, maintained that he helped thousands of people regain their health simply through the use of positive self-suggestion. He helped sick people by planting positive suggestions that their health was improving. His apparent success rate was so high that a whole movement developed which was based upon his ideas of self-suggestion.

Positive suggestion is particularly important in the development of a child. Too often a child's weaknesses and inabilities are stressed during education. A weakness or inability usually only exists through lack of training and attention rather than through actual physiological lack. All children should be encouraged by giving them a positive set. And it is sad to reflect on how many great minds and ideas must have been lost through lack of encouragement and positive suggestion. The positive use of language helps everyone to demonstrate to themselves and to others that they are capable. Therefore, always plant positive memory seeds in your own mind and in other people's.

Negative thinking and pessimistic outlook

When was the last time you worried about work, or money, or the family, or yourself? When was the last time you felt depressed? When was the last time you started asking yourself the 'what if . . .' type of question? That sort of question predicts disaster, and is caused by negative thinking and outlook. Whenever you start to think negatively you are more likely to notice negative information to support your negative thinking. Much of what you perceive is merely a reflection of what is going on in your head. Some people spend so much time reviewing their negative store that their ability to discuss negative ideas seems exhaustive — the sort of person who keeps saying, 'What if there is another energy crisis?', or, 'What if I become ill?'

There is always a great temptation when you come across somebody, or indeed yourself, thinking negatively, to simply say 'stop it'. However, it is not that easy to stop thinking in a particular way because if you try to stop yourself thinking something it often has the opposite effect. For example, consciously trying to go to sleep only tends to make you wake up. It is rather like telling someone that he will win ten thousand pounds if he can spend a whole minute without thinking about the word 'abracadabra'! Because he is *not* meant to think about it, he will inevitably think about it and so not win the ten thousand pounds! The way to temporarily stop yourself thinking along particularly negative lines is to get actively involved in something else. However, this is only a short-term measure and in the long run may not be sufficient. There are two ways to help reduce negative thinking and outlook, the first is analysis and the second is the use of imagery.

116

1 Objective analysis

Negative ideas must be challenged. The first question to ask is, 'Is it rational?' Analyse the ideas, worries or problems and then, if appropriate, decide on a course of action and carry it out. Realise that you have done everything possible in relation to that problem and then you can stop thinking about it.

Problems make people tense and irritable. The way that they have overcome various problems and situations in the past tends to make them conditioned to worry. Given a problem you may automatically start worrying. This is an example of a very basic sort of memory. The problem equals a stimulus and your worry equals the response. Instead of becoming tuned up and ready for rational thinking and action you tend to become muddleheaded and unthinking, and so you are far less able to solve any problem! In extreme cases people may feel totally unable to solve any problem unless they actually do worry about it! This is because whenever they have solved a problem in the past they have worried about it. Therefore, they think that if they do not worry the problem will not be solved! To break this condition, and reflex, you need to analyse your problem. You will then be able to decide if your tension is rational. Nearly always you will find that by looking at the problem and tension separately you can overcome both through the use of objective analysis.

Another characteristic of negative thinking is the way people stress their mistakes. By stressing and dwelling upon your mistakes you tend to make them easier to repeat. Dwelling upon your mistakes erodes your confidence, and even increases your chances of repeating the mistake. It is essential to realise that whenever you learn anything you learn it by trial and error. The error is an essential part of learning. You learn how to ride a bicycle by learning how not to fall off. However, many people think that if they make a mistake it is a reason for giving up and accepting defeat. The mistake then becomes more important than what they were trying to do, and quickly becomes an obsession. This sort of obsession can even cause a cyclic memory pattern; that is, you start to believe that simply because something has happened in the past it is going to happen again in the future. You must think rationally in this situation. It is not enough to think that the root of your problem is irrational, you must genuinely convince yourself that it is irrational and then you will be able to stop thinking about it.

2 Imagery

Negative imagery, that is, a negative picture in your mind, has a great effect upon your performance. The reason for this is that the picture, the image, is a very basic language. It is the language you knew first. You could see and remember images before you learnt verbal language. Although you may be able to reason away, or solve, a problem, you may still be left with negative imagery in your mind.

By using positive analysis you will find that much of your negative thinking and negative stress is reduced. However, strongly negative situations tend to cause the imagination to run riot.

Similar to the situation of worry, you find that simply by deciding to stop seeing negative images you will not successfully control your imagination. If anything the images will increase. The way to reduce negative imagery is to introduce positive imagery. Do not dwell upon the negative images simply introduce a massive dose of positive images. If the images concern a particular problem, introduce positive images which show you solving the problem. If the negative images are concerned with a particular fear, introduce positive images which show you overcoming the fears. You will find that by doing this, your positive memory will always win, and as a result, the positive memories and images will give you a positive set, which, because of your self-proving ability, you

118

will be inclined to confirm. Therefore, whenever you recall a negative idea or image let it be an alarm bell and inject a massive quantity of positive and enjoyable image memories.

And so to summarise: firstly analyse your memories. Decide if there is any rational basis for the problem, and if there is no rational basis decide with genuine feeling that the idea is unreasonable and, therefore, not part of you. Then flood out negative memories with positive and pleasurable memories.

The more times you play over a memory the more you remember it as you review it each time. Do not play back a lot of negative memories, they cause depression, pessimistic daydreaming, tension, worry, fear, or simply a rather gloomy outlook, and will tend to obsess your conscious mind.

Always ensure a positive set and positive images. Play only a positive tape and see only the positive around you.

Unproductive use of memory

It is possible to become prejudiced by being over-set in one area of information. This type of mental set will only absorb information which confirms existing information and practically ignores all other conflicting ideas. Fanatics and extremists of all kinds suffer from over-set.

You always need to be aware that in adopting a set you automatically increase your ability to tune into that type of information and you also reduce your awareness and acceptance of other information. Therefore, you are easily inclined to reject information which does not agree or fit into your mental set. The danger can, therefore, be that, as such a person gets older, he or she becomes progressively more mentally inflexible. This person will often see and justify his point of view in an absolute and over-simplified concept of Right and Wrong and perhaps even refuse to tolerate any form of discussion. A prejudiced person will over-react to rational argument and become emotional, or angry, in self-defence.

Through understanding the effect of any set you become more aware of the dangers in over-belief or self-righteousness. The prejudiced tend to believe that the information is part and parcel of their person and that an attack on that information is a personal attack. This can generate the idea that the information which they 'possess' is right and that the more information they 'possess' the more right they are.

Information and knowledge are generally available to everyone. Only rarely can you say you actually 'possess' knowledge, in the sense that you alone are the owner of it. Also, it is very rarely that you can say that information or knowledge is absolutely right or wrong. Information should be used as a constructive tool, available to everyone to help them develop and understand themselves and their environment.

All too often information is simply respected for its own sake. A person who is an 'expert' often uses information in the same way that a boxer uses his muscle power: by trying to knock the living daylights out of other experts by slugging information blows. This pastime is no more civilised than any other animal conflict. You could say that these 'experts' are more ignorant than a child who at least has the ability to discuss and develop new areas of knowledge. The child is still able to evaluate information.

Throughout your life your ideas will have changed and they will probably continue to do so. As you absorb new information your views tend to keep changing. The more you learn and remember the more you become aware of the mass of information you do not know. An expert, who is using information constructively, will very often be exceptionally undogmatic, being tolerant and receptive to new ideas. He recognises that there is so much he does not know that he can rarely be dogmatic about anything. Furthermore, he has discovered that the greater his knowledge and memory, the more he needs to qualify a new fact or idea. This flexible

120

approach allows the person to use his information in a purposeful and constructive way, and rarely do you find that such a person holds intractable views.

A useful method of testing your own set is to adopt the set of another person, especially a person with whom you disagree. Try arguing, try accepting information from a completely new standpoint. As a result of this you will often find that you adopt a wider, more integrated viewpoint. The wider your point of view, the greater your ability will be to receive fresh information.

Alternative set, that is, the method of adopting the other person's set in cases of disagreement, is useful in many different situations. Take a simple domestic situation of husband and wife who have both gradually adopted the set that the other is selfish. They will accordingly notice the selfish rather than the selfless behaviour of their partner. They therefore remember only the selfish behaviour and so again become increasingly aware of it until they can see only selfishness. In this case the husband and/or wife could well adopt one or both of the following two sets:

1 Ways in which he or she is selfless.
2 Ways in which I am selfish.

Very quickly the person would find that the selfishness was not as 'real' as originally thought. In all aspects of life your memories very radically affect your attitudes and in turn your behaviour.

You have seen that the word 'but' encourages negative comment and will often indicate that you are using information as a muscle to pull a punch rather than as a constructive force. If two people talk and each one keeps 'but'ing the other, the conversation will rarely be productive, and often break down. This affect can be illustrated by the analogy of the see-saw. Each person tries to out-balance the weight of his opposition, until finally the see-saw itself breaks

121

— in other words the corridor of communication — and the conversation snaps.

The use of the word 'but' is usually an indication that you are preparing your ideas while the other speaker is still talking, without giving full attention to what is being said. This encourages you to prejudge the conversation and to fail to 'listen creatively'. The ability to listen creatively is helped if you put yourself in the place of the person who is talking. Whenever they stop talking you try and creatively continue whatever it was they were saying. Often this effect can be achieved by '*and*'ing and not 'but'ing. Creative listening helps you to take in fresh information and ideas and not simply to run through your own information like a record stuck in one groove.

Static memory

Imagine two people walking along a river bank at dawn. The river runs through a rich valley. Sunlight is just starting to pour down into the valley and is glinting on the water's surface. A cluster of lilies are bobbing up and down in the water, their flowers brilliant white in the fresh light.

The first person sees the lilies, registers the word 'lily' in his mind then moves on. The second person sees the lily cluster, stops to observe the lilies, noting new shades and textures and whole new appearances previously unseen. The first person relied on static memory; he saw, referred to his pre-existing categories, and then dismissed — 'static memory' stops you from appreciating afresh.

Your pre-established memory can stop you from learning anything new about your surroundings. Try, the next time you see a flower, or any natural object, to stare at it. Just look at it. To begin with you may feel that you are wasting your time. You may feel that you know everything there is to know about a flower, perhaps a rose. However, keep looking. Soon

you will begin to notice new details in the rose — a special colour, a particular shape, an inter-locking structure — many things otherwise unseen. You may not have seen these new aspects before because your pre-established memory of a rose did not allow for new observation. If you keep looking at the rose you will learn more and more and, as with any information, the more you understand the more you will know that there is even more to understand! This 'full' look method helps you see anything and everything with new and fuller awareness, and can help you to taste more, hear more, feel more, smell more and so on.

Static memory is rather like static water — it stagnates. For your awareness to develop you need fresh and changing memories — not a single static memory which limits your perception and appreciation.

Static words and ideas

Many words you use are simple verbal tags. For example, a lily is not the word lily — it is the actual plant. Verbal tags are used for convenience in communication, but they can lead to a lack of fresh appraisal.

Verbal tags create difficulties in communication between adults and children. A child who has spent a happy day at the sea may be disinclined to talk about it later. No matter how much he or she enjoyed it, the child finds that words cannot sufficiently describe the colour and splendour of the experience. And so the child will remain silent. The child's world is more 'real', more colourful; whereas the adult world is more verbal. The word for the child is an inadequate tag whereas the word for the adult is very often the only tag.

Word tags are very personal. The words 'Communist' and 'God' have very different memory associations and connections from person to person. The word 'Communist' in some people's minds means 'anti-American, anti-democratic, oppressive, dictatorial', whereas others interpret it to mean 'universal equality, ultimate democracy, peaceful co-existence, harmony'. The realisation that people understand words in different ways can give a new insight into the nature of many disagreements, and so hopefully to avoid these disagreements; it is simply a question of memory associations! By realising that people remember words and ideas in a highly

124

individual way, disagreements and poor communications can often be overcome.

Words and ideas can all too easily become static. If you have a particular pet idea it can be very difficult not to resent a new idea which disagrees with your idea. Everyone suffers from a degree of 'misoneism', that is an unreasoning fear and hatred of new ideas, especially when the ideas contradict your own ideas and whole way of thinking. Whenever you find yourself unwilling to accept new information, check yourself for 'static memory'. A very good example of misoneism was the public opposition to the acceptance of Darwin's *The Origin of Species*, epitomised in the trial of an American schoolteacher in 1925 simply for teaching Darwin's theory of evolution! To have accepted the new theory of evolution they would have had to totally recategorise and re-think their ideas and memory links.

All of us tend to ascribe meanings to certain words and ideas that do not necessarily exist. For example, Carl Jung coined the words 'extrovert' and 'introvert', and as a result people have since developed definite ideas of what an introvert or extrovert person is like. However, these words are simple absolutes. They represent extremes in a classification scale which were simply thought up in one man's mind. Because the words are accepted, people actually believe in the terms as though they are real. It is of course impossible to divide people into two such simplistic types, but it is easy to slip into the habit of thinking in rigid, compartmentalised extremes.

To overcome this static 'absolute' tendency, you need to reappraise — in the same way as when looking at the rose — what you understand by a particular word. On a verbal level, simply say the word over and over again until you find it becomes increasingly difficult to say and understand. By doing this you achieve an effect which is known as 'verbal satiation'. Take the phrase 'yellow-bellied liar' and say it thirty times. Having done that you will notice two things —

firstly that it becomes difficult and strange to say and secondly that you have many different thoughts about the phrase and so make new memory associations.

On a mental level it is advisable to 'out think' an idea. To do this, keep turning over a particular idea in your mind, considering it from as many different viewpoints as possible. This will give many new aspects to the idea, in the same way that you saw many different aspects to the rose. This sort of verbal, and especially mental, exercise will help you to become more aware of words as a means of communication rather than as an end in themselves with a set and absolute meaning.

As an example of how a particular word may have forced you to think in a particular way, consider the question, 'What is the point of life?'

One man might think, 'What is the *point* of life?' If he finds a *point* he may be very happy. If he fails to find any *point* he may become unhappy.

Another man might think beyond the question. He would immediately see that there is a presumption that there is such a thing as a 'point' to life. The first man, like Western man, is very inclined to want to find points, causes, reasons and effects. The second man is not concerned about a 'point' to life, however, this does not mean that he is depressed. The sentence had little meaning for him as the word 'point' had not created a concept or need for the concept 'point' in his mind. Therefore, if you tell him that there is no point to life it is of no consequence.

If you find that you cannot accept the stand of the second man — in other words you insist there is a point to life — from the second man's point of view you are caught in your own words, your memory of those words. The word 'point' has created an idea around which you have built up a complex of ideas and reasons. The word 'point' has actually created a reality in your mind. It can be very difficult to think beyond this complex structure.

Summary

X When the mind is given a 'set' it notices information to support that set. The set actually reduces the ability to recognise information that disagrees with that 'set'

X The 'set' — whether positive or negative — constantly reinforces itself

X Negative set indicators include: negative language (but), negative suggestion (have you had a car accident *yet*), negative thinking (what if?) and pessimistic outlook. Reduce the last two, firstly by objective analysis, then introduce positive imagery

X The self-proving tendency will confirm the positive set and imagery

X To avoid becoming overset try adopting the opposite set of beliefs. Avoid the 'expert' role of information boxer

X Listen creatively *and* try 'and'ing

X Use the 'full' look method to stop static memory of what you perceive, say and think. Stop words taking on an absolute meaning by using the full say and think method

5 Images

For a long time it was thought that it was the eyes and not the brain that saw images. However, it was noticed that if the brain was injured, and the eyes remained intact, a person could become blind.

Vision works through the eye gathering and focusing light into images on the back wall of the eye, which is called the retina. Sensitive cells in the retina then convert the energy of light into signals which are transmitted to the brain. The brain converts these signals into what is 'perceived'.

After-images

There are certain visual effects which are sometimes confused with the idea of photographic memory — these are the immediate short-term effects perceived after looking at something and are called positive and negative after-images.

Positive and negative after-images

If you look at a bright colour and then look away for a short time, afterwards you may continue to see the same colour and shape. If you look at a bright light, for a short time afterwards you may continue to see the same intense light even though **you are looking away. Although the actual light source has** gone, there is continued activity in the cells at the back of the eye. Although the source has gone the eye remains stimulated.

The effect can occur when driving at night behind another car. If you have been staring at the car in front you may notice that when you suddenly move your eyes to one side you continue to see the number plate of the car in front, even though you are no longer looking at it. Usually this image will only remain for a fraction of a second.

Following the positive image there may occur a negative after-image. This is more commonly experienced. Try looking at the dot in the blue circle on the front cover of this book. Concentrate on that dot for at least thirty seconds, and then look at the dot in the white square on the back.

What do you see? For a few moments nothing may happen and then you may see a coloured circle. Having looked at the blue circle the circle you see may well be yellow, however the yellow outline may be blue. The negative after-image becomes the colour that is described as complimentary to the original colour. This negative image is caused because the light-sensitive cells are exhausted temporarily. Like positive after-images, negative after-images quickly disappear and cannot be reseen as can 'memory' images.

You will notice that these after-images move when you move your eyes, which indicates that they are not strictly a memory but the after effect of a lasting stimulation on the eye itself. Similarly, other experiences can appear to continue after the particular stimulation has ceased; for example, if you have been travelling by sea you may continue to feel as if you are rolling about for some time after you are back on land.

After-images will also vary in size according to the distance of the surface onto which your eye projects them. Look at the coloured circles for another thirty seconds. Then look at the white square with the dot. Once you start to see the after-

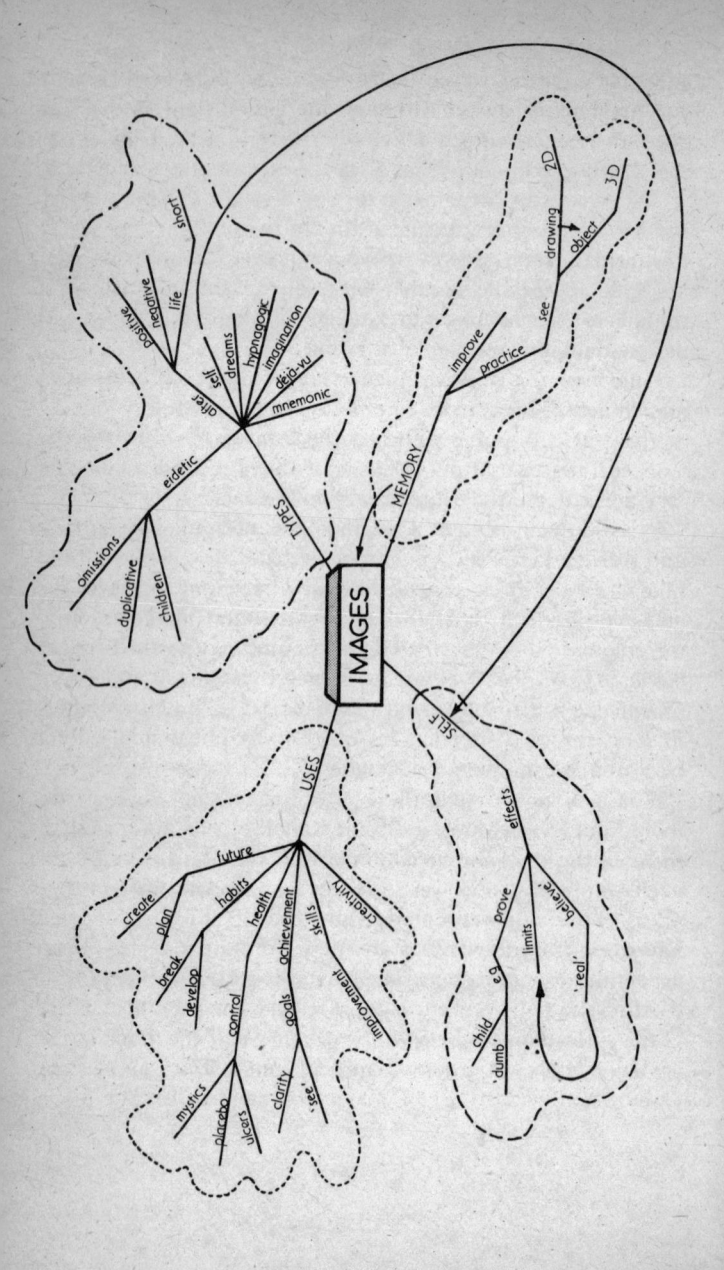

image move the book to and from your eyes. You may see the circle changing in size. These two characteristics are common to the after-image and not the memory image.

Photographic (eidetic) memory

'Photographic memory' is the term commonly used to describe a remarkable ability, possessed by some people, of reproducing images they have seen in the past. Eidetic (meaning duplicative) is the scientific term.

Eidetic memory is more often found in children than in adults. Whereas only up to 10 per cent of adults possess this ability up to 60 per cent of children under eleven can reproduce images in this way.

Look closely at the illustration on the following page of 'the death of Sherlock Holmes and Moriarty'. Spend at least a minute looking at it.

The person with eidetic-memory ability can see this picture even though he or she looks away. The picture will appear to be outside their heads. It will appear to be in front of them hanging in space. They can continue to look at the picture after it has gone and their eyes actually scan the picture in looking at the detail. Whereas the after-image disappeared after a short while, this memory image (eidetic image) can be conjured up at will later on.

While our after-image varies in size according to the distance of the surface on which the image is seen, the eidetic image remains approximately the same size regardless of the change in distance of the viewing surface.

There are certain indications that this memory ability is not so much photographic as reproductive. It is unlikely that the mind is actually re-seeing the same picture. The brain seems to reassemble the various parts of the picture. The recalled image may not be 100 per cent accurate; there may be certain omissions and there may be certain distortions. Children, for

SIDNEY PAGET
1893

132

example, may miss out those bits of the pictures which are of no particular interest to them.

Another interesting aspect is that the mind will tend to complete the picture. The remembered image of this illustration might well show how Sherlock Holmes survived!

Visual memory development

The degree of visual memory and image ability varies from person to person. In the case of eidetic memory there tends to be a much greater richness of original detail than in the more usually experienced memory image. People involved in work or interests requiring visual awareness often have a better visual memory than average. Artists, surgeons and architects develop good visual memories.

Most people can improve their visual memory by exercising their visual awareness. Take a simple object, perhaps something like a book or a vase. Draw a clear and simple picture of that object. Study this two dimensional drawing for at least five minutes a day. Look closely at the drawing, observe all the detail in the drawing and then close your eyes and try to re-see as much of it as possible. When you have a good image of the drawing start looking at the object itself. Make sure that you look at the object from the same angle from which it was drawn. Once again, look at it, paying attention to detail, and then try and see it clearly in your mind's eye. Slowly you will experience a gradual increase in your visual memory of that object. This practice needs to be done at least once a day. Even if you can spare only one or two minutes a day, it is much better to practise little and often rather than for long periods only occasionally.

You will find that the object does become clear in your mind's eye. Some people, having reached this stage, can actually project the image at will onto or into their everyday surroundings. This is very similar to the eidetic ability. This type of visual exercise improves the whole visual memory.

Hypnagogic images

Occasionally a person may think that they never experience any form of imagery. They may think that they only ever remember in words. However, such people may experience imagery in their dreams. Also, people who say they do not see images can see how a word is written if they close their eyes and imagine the word. This is an example of imagery.

People experience very vivid images just before falling asleep. This state is called hypnagogic imaging. Usually, people have no control over this sort of imaging. These images have been used by various artists and writers to provide inspiration: Blake, Coleridge and Enid Blyton all referred to this state as a source of ideas and inspiration. Scientists, too, have claimed flashes of insight in this state; for example, the structure of the benzine molecule was first 'seen', by the Frenchman, Kekulé, just as he was going to sleep.

Déjà vû

You may have had the experience from time to time of feeling that you have lived through a situation before. On arriving in a certain town, or going into a room, you may feel quite convinced that you have been there before and already experienced what is happening to you. You feel that everything is terribly familiar and yet you cannot quite remember what is going to happen next. This experience is usually called *déjà vû* (meaning 'already seen'). Although in an extreme form *déjà vû* can be an indication of a particular brain dysfunction, it is nearly always an entirely harmless and fascinating phenomenon.

One likely explanation of *déjà vû* is that your senses simply perceive the similarities between something new and

134

something remembered. If you are walking down a street your senses will be recording all sorts of information. If enough of your senses are picking up past associations then together they may put two and two together and make five; leading you to believe that you have been there before. The Greek philosopher, Plato, believed that this particular experience was evidence to indicate a previous incarnation — as indeed do some religions today.

The use of imagery

Some people make very individual connections and associations with their images. Often they bear little relation to the images. For example, one person might think of the days of the week as representing a particular colour; others have a particular image for each month of the year — when they hear or say the name of a particular month they automatically see the same image. This type of basic image association is probably developed early on in life.

The ability to use imagery — to combine images in an original way and to mix the images of all your senses — is the foundation of much artistic and creative ability. To realise how imaginative you are, try to manipulate the following images. Firstly, read through the sequence of images, and then close your eyes and see each individual step in the sequence.

1 See a very large frog.
2 See the frog jumping from the earth to the moon.
3 See the frog eating the moon.
4 See the frog jumping back to the earth.

In seeing those images you are relying on visual memories that you have already stored, and you are using those visual memories in a highly imaginative and creatively original way.

As well as manipulating images to help create novel ideas, images should be used to practise physical skills. Sportsmen instinctively use this technique. A basketball player may run through the mental images which show him scoring goals. Research shows that such mental practice can actually improve performance. Tennis players or golfers frequently close their eyes and concentrate while they mentally rehearse certain strokes or shots. A mental run-through will often improve performance. In the same way that the reviewing of information reinforces the memory, the 'imaging' of a skill can reinforce the memory traces controlling the activity and so make the imaged action more spontaneous. Try a mental run-through and see how your performance improves.

Self-image

People generally have some idea of what they are like — they have some kind of 'self-image'. If you see yourself as being particularly good at something you will actually tend to be good at it, and if you see yourself as bad at something you will tend to be bad at it. This image, although often vague, affects your performance. People tend to act in accordance with the self-image they have of themselves.

Your self-image works in much the same way as your self-proving ability. Unless you have a fairly clear self-image other people can easily affect your own image and therefore hamper your development. The self-memory or image is rather like a form of self-hypnosis, that is you will do things that you believe that you can do, and you will tend to not do those things you believe you cannot do. If a heavyweight boxer is hypnotised into believing that he is incapable of lifting up his right arm he will subsequently be incapable of lifting that arm. No matter how much he sweats and strains he just cannot lift the arm. This shows that the subconscious mind is a very strong force. If it believes that something is true it will tend to act in accordance with that belief. The important point to note is that the subconscious mind is influenced by images held in the mind. The image is a very basic language to all animals. Man learnt how to see a long time before he learnt how to speak. This natural language shows itself in dreams and in your everyday imagination.

The **strength** of the subconscious mind is illustrated well in the case of a female Olympic high jumper who injured her heel while jumping. Following the injury she was incapable of jumping as well as before. It was noticed that after the accident she jumped in a slightly different way, indicating that she was afraid of injuring herself again. She agreed to allow herself to be hypnotised into believing that she could safely jump as she used to. Having been hypnotised she found that she could not only jump as well as before but, in fact, better. Prior to hypnotism she had wanted and willed herself to achieve her previous standard but without effect. The will of the conscious mind was subordinate to the subconscious mind.

The subconscious mind can be directed through the use of images and make you tend to act in accordance with the memory images you have of yourself and so make the images 'real'. Emile Coué, recognising the strength of the imagination over will-power, encouraged his patients always to 'see' themselves as being better.

In the same way that the 'set' you have encourages you to notice certain information, the images you stress and hold in your everyday life, and so constantly review, encourage you to notice information that links to and supports those images. And because of your self-proving tendency you will tend to act so as to confirm your images. If you hold predominantly negative images in your mind, for example images of inability, you probably will find that you do not succeed because you start to believe that the images are true. And so not only does a pre-set, or an image, affect the information you absorb, the pre-set and image can affect your everyday performance.

Images and achievements

When walking down a very crowded street, you will have noticed that if you are just meandering along you are buffeted and barged into and make only slow progress. However, if you look ahead and purposefully pick a particular spot that you want to reach, you find that you can much more quickly weave your way through the oncoming crowd. This analogy helps you understand the concept of using an image to help achieve an objective. Very few people ever decide exactly what they want to achieve. Rather like a person in a crowd they tend to meander along. However, if you decide on your objective and give your mind a definite image which shows you achieving it, you will find it is much easier to get where you want to be.

The image forces you to clarify your objectives and, providing it is clear and positive, automatically makes the task much easier because the mind is set to notice any opportunities which help achieve those objectives. Therefore, there are two requirements: you must really decide what event or result you want to achieve; then you need to see your achievement clearly and regularly remind yourself of that image, so that it is firmly ingrained in your mind.

If you see and believe in yourself as successful you will tend to succeed. Again, it is a good idea to use all the senses in visualising this personal achievement, because by using all of them your planned objective will become more real and your mind more set.

You can further encourage definite achievement images by acting as if you have already achieved your goal. Feel the success, encourage the ambition and clearly see yourself achieving the goal.

You may feel that the use of these memorised images is rather like programming a computer to react in a certain way.

138

The analogy is valid. However, you may feel that you do not want to be programmed! It is important to realise that people are being programmed by themselves all the time with images — thousands of images and suggestions from various sources — and that these images and suggestions are very often negative. This is why it can be difficult to achieve anything. Negative images always tend to reduce confidence and without confidence one is inclined to be inactive, or at least ineffective. If you are inactive there is little chance of making any headway whatsoever.

The image has always been recognised as a great source of strength and power. Ancient idols and religious images have always been used to encourage and develop particular abilities and characteristics. Religious teachers have relied upon the parable which is an image story form, because they found them by far the most effective way of communicating ideas. Prayer is itself a constant reminder to the human brain of a religious direction.

To sum up, make sure that you encourage success images and avoid negative images. When a negative image occurs to you, flood it out with a positive image. Rather than floundering around in a mass of conflicting and often negative images, give yourself a few definite success images and you will find that you automatically start to achieve your desired ends.

Images and health

Emile Coué maintained that a person's health could be improved through positive suggestion. He also found that images affect health. Western medicine increasingly recognises that processes like heart beat, glandular excretion and healing, which used to be thought of as automatic, can be consciously controlled. Some people, for example, can immediately increase their heart beat by vividly imagining themselves running. You may be able to increase the temperature of your hand by imagining that you are holding a red hot poker, or reduce its temperture by imagining that you are putting it in a bucket of freezing water.

Positive images and positive suggestions affect the mind in similar ways. Both tend to encourage a person to believe in the truth of the suggestion or image. This belief affects a person's whole performance and well being.

A placebo — a dummy pill or substance which has no pharmacological property and therefore should not affect a patient's health — when prescribed by a doctor will often cause a marked improvement in health, providing the patient believes that the pill is genuine. This shows that a person's belief and attitude will affect their health.

Many experiments, involving thousands of people, have demonstrated under laboratory conditions that it is possible to control heart beat, blood pressure and body temperature, at will. Yogis and mystics for thousands of years have consciously controlled their pain thresholds, enabling them to walk over red-hot coals and otherwise tolerate what for most people would be impossibly painful experiences.

While few of us ever test our will to the extent of the yogi, we can allow memory images to affect our health — both for better or for worse. In middle age a man has a choice: he can see himself as ageing and so decide not to overdo things; he therefore remains fairly inactive in order to preserve himself. Or he can see himself as fit and lively as ever, and expect nothing but good health. Medically, there may be little difference between these two men, yet the first may tend to go into hibernation in an unnaturally sedentary way, while the second remains fully active and continues to exercise. As a result he feels well, acts well, and so encourages well being, while the other, imitating the life of a fragile fossil, starts to resemble one. And so you see that the self-image can cause a very marked physical difference through change in behaviour.

In extreme cases ideas and mental images can adversely affect health. The most extreme example is that of the tribal witch doctor who can kill by instilling in the mind the belief and image that a person will die. To a lesser extent, retirement can affect people just as tragically. Where before the person had some sense of purpose, having retired he may have little purpose and his health can quickly collapse.

The phenomenon of stigmata, that is where a change occurs in the body through concentrating on a particular characteristic, is well documented in Christianity. Allegedly St Francis of Assisi developed sympathetic scar wounds on his hands because he had dwelt upon the image of the crucifixion for such a long time. More and more doctors recognise that many illnesses have a psychosomatic (mind over body) origin. An obvious example of such an effect is when an executive under stress develops duodenal ulcers. It is also interesting to note that psychiatric patients tend to have more illnesses than other people.

The image can be used to programme the mind with an expectation of health. Although it is not entirely clear how the brain directly affects the body, it is known that the image can have an immediate effect over the body and furthermore that the image will cause a person to act in such a way as to encourage the realisation of that image.

Images and habits

When you have tried to break a habit you may have found that the more you wanted to stop, the more persistent the habit became. For example, if you have decided to try a weight-reducing diet you may all too easily have finished before you started the diet! The reason for this is quite simple. When you want to stop doing something you usually see or imagine yourself doing the activity you wish to stop, therefore the more you want to stop doing something the more images you produce of yourself doing that act.

It is always easier to carry something through if you have already seen yourself doing it. So simply wanting to get out of a particular habit is not enough. People are strongly affected by images; if you are in a theatre where you are not allowed to smoke and during the play one of the actors lights up a cigarette, you can accidentally light a cigarette yourself. It is because the image has such a powerful effect that so much money is spent on advertising.

To break a habit, simply plant an image of yourself *not* doing the habit and doing something else instead. For example, if you want to lose weight, you might see yourself as being thin and also see yourself eating alternative suitable foods. Or, if you want to stop smoking, you should picture yourself refusing a cigarette with ease, and at the same time involved in some other activity. Those who have given up smoking will know the image strength of an advertisement for cigarettes; the image of someone smoking quickly makes you want to imitate.

On the other hand there may be certain habits that you want to adopt. In this case make a clear image in your mind of the habit you want to develop and simply see yourself developing the habit.

Images and 'future memory' patterns

The memory pattern can be used to set yourself certain target images. By programming definite memory images into your brain you can literally create a future. In doing this you are developing what is called future memory! You can use this future memory pattern for immediate and long-term achievement. Each day you can produce a memory pattern of everything you want to achieve during the day. Having constructed the pattern you then run through the various images and see yourself performing the desired acts.

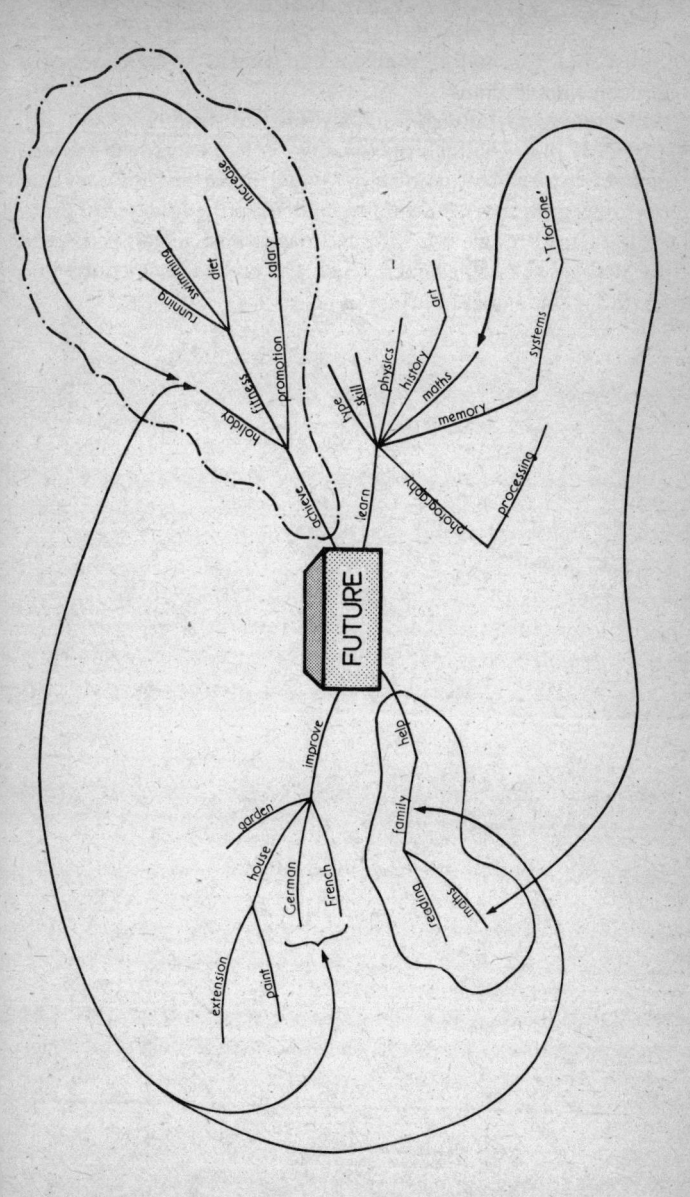

Subsequently, you find that it is much easier to carry out your predetermined plans.

A long-term pattern can be built up gradually and will probably only change occasionally. This pattern will include images of all the situations that you are working towards and the objectives that you want to achieve in the long term. Once a day run through the various images and visualise the end result; feel the achievement. The pattern will soon turn into perfectly remembered future images.

Summary

X Positive after-images are caused by continued activity in the cells at the back of the eye after the light source has been removed. Negative after-images occur because the light sensitive cells are temporarily exhausted

X Eidetic memory ability is more often found in children than in adults. This ability resembles 'photographic' memory

X Visual memory can be developed through the practice of trying to remember visually a definite object

X Vivid imagery, called hypnagogic imaging, occurs on falling asleep

X *Déjà vû*, a sense of familiarity, may be caused because the brain receives stimuli very similar to previous stimuli

X Imagery can be used to practise a skill or sport

X The self-image, like the self-proving ability, tends to dictate the possible behaviour of an individual. This image is rather like a form of self-hypnosis and affects the whole mind

X Definite achievement images make a person clarify his aims. The image encourages the self-proving ability to achieve the image

X Western medicine increasingly recognises the control of the mind over the body. The image can be used to programme the mind for health

X The imagination often proves to be stronger than the conscious will. Images can therefore be used to break unwanted habits

X Specific images can be used to plan and help achieve future goals

6   And So Now . . .

Perfect memory? — Retrieval pattern — Memory and:
creativity, imagination, intelligence, comprehension —
Effects of memory development

By now you should have come to the conclusion that your
memories are inseparable from *you* as an individual. Memory,
which you may have assumed to be a natural and simple
ability, has been shown to be unimaginably complex.

Perfect memory?

There is an impressive body of research which suggests that
the human brain may record all experience. Chapter 1
referred to Dr Penfield's research. Dr Penfield stimulated the
brain with minute electrodes and found that his patients re-
experienced events from early on in their lives with great
clarity. For example, if my brain were stimulated by an
electrode five years from now I might totally re-experience
writing this sentence again. This means that all your
yesterdays may be stored ready for playback if stimulated
correctly.

You have probably experienced moments when your
memory proved itself to be better than you thought. But could
it possibly be perfect?

Walking along you may suddenly capture a particular smell
or sight or hear a sound — perhaps some music — that
triggers off a whole realm of previously forgotten memories. A
particular profile of a face, a turn of phrase or a particular

146

intonation, the half smile on someone's lips — these sort of events can suddenly bring back the past.

If I ask you, 'What were you doing five years ago today?', you may have absolutely no idea. However, if there is an entry in your diary for that day, I might be able, by reading just two words from it, to bring back most of the original detail.

Memory is not so much a question of storage, more one of retrieval, a question of being able to find the appropriate links and cues leading back to the stored information.

A person under hypnosis is often able to recall whole areas of their lives previously thought forgotten. Such a hypnotised subject may remember vocabulary and expressions that he used as a child but has subsequently been unable to remember. A hypnotised person is more susceptible to suggestion and his mind allows fairly free-flowing association. This freer associative ability is important in allowing old connections and links to be fully re-established.

The use of free association is the underlying idea behind the truth drug, sodium pentothal, which simply encourages a person to be more naturally and spontaneously associative and so makes him 'spill the beans'.

Another subjective experience which suggests perfect memory is the 'death-type experience'. A person who has survived a moment when he believed he was about to die, very often claims that: 'My whole life flashed in front of me'. Those who have had this experience describe it as though the whole of their life did actually flash before their eyes, as if the whole of their life was given a final review!

Your own dreams may sometimes include detail which you thought was lost. The clarity of such detail, especially in a lucid dream, can be remarkable. An old person may begin to dream about childhood friends not seen or thought of for sixty or seventy years. You may have noticed that although some older people's recent memory is not good, their recall of childhood is fairly precise. An old person may not even be able

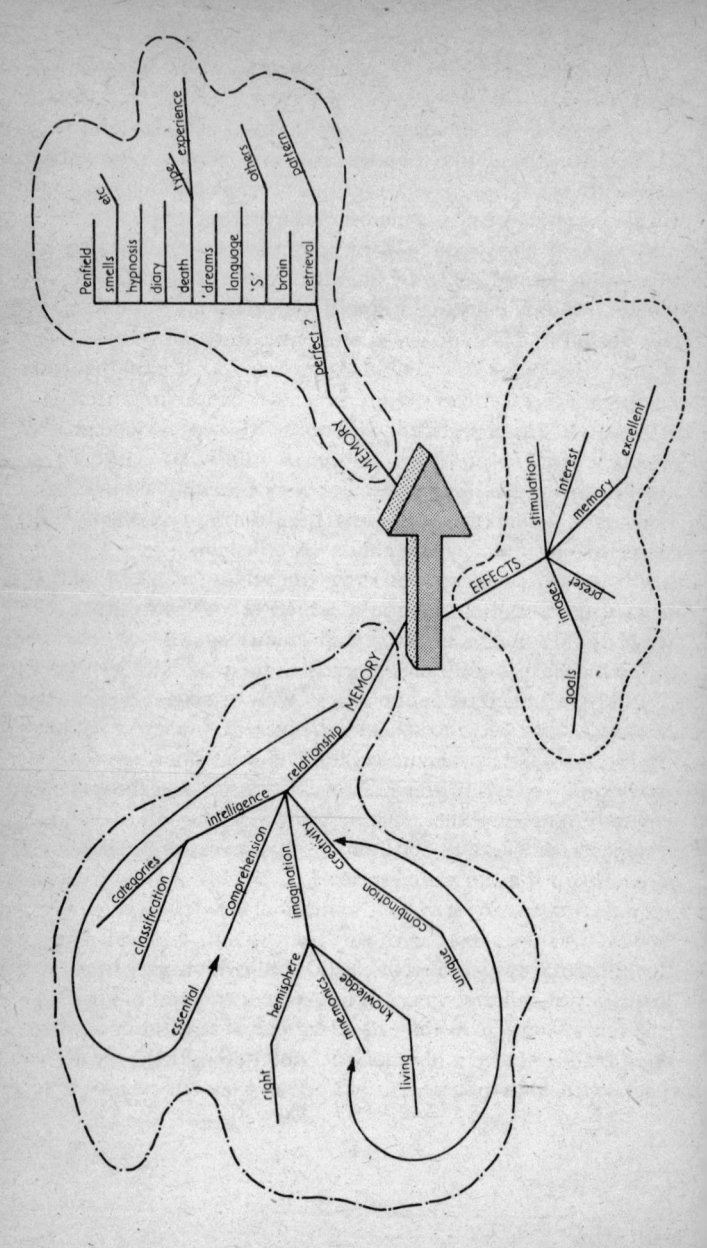

to remember what he had for lunch (or even whether or not he has already had lunch!) but he can remember childhood adventures and places with crystal clarity.

The storage capacity of the brain is effectively limitless, and there are some people who seem to be able to store and recall nearly all information. One famous example was the Russian journalist known as 'S'. The editor in charge of 'S' could not understand why everyone else took written notes. 'S' did not need any form of written record — he simply remembered. 'S' was studied by the Russian psychologist, Professor A. R. Luria. His book, *The Mind of a Mnemonist*, describes his study of this remarkable man. 'S' 's memory was so complete that if asked the question, 'What were you doing five years ago today?' he was likely to answer, 'At what time?'

'S' 's problem was not one of memory but of not being able to forget! It is interesting to note that the only way he could forget effectively was to completely believe in his ability to do so. Only when he did this, did he actually manage to forget. Again you see that belief and confidence play a vital role in remembering and forgetting!

There have been other people renowned for remarkable recall abilities. To mention just a few of them: Themistocles remembered the 20,000 names of the citizens of Athens; Xerxes was supposed to be able to remember the 100,000 names of his army; Ben Jonson is said to have remembered everything he wrote; Paul Morphy, the chess player, remembered every chess move he had ever made. All these people provide impressive evidence to suggest that everyone possesses exceptional memory abilities.

However, you do not simply want to cram your mind full of useless information. Einstein said, 'Why should I clutter up my mind with facts when I have a perfectly good library?' To fill one's mind with a mass of disconnected information is simply to become an idiot *savant*. Information is largely for use and not for show.

Memory systems are also evidence of people's untapped memory resources. Greek orators who were masters of mnemonics could make a speech with no notes whatsoever, lasting for several hours. The 'T for one' system can be used by anyone to remember thousands of facts or figures. The mnemonist who astounds his audience with his feats of memory is only demonstrating an ability you already have.

Retrieval pattern

Very often your mind needs time to re-establish connections. To help yourself try and remember anything, firstly think around the subject you wish to remember and then simply leave it. You will often find that the answer literally springs to mind as a result. The memory pattern can be well used in this retrieval task. Draw a memory pattern with a blank centre to represent the missing information. Around the centre you put down any information you can think of which relates to that missing centre. For example, if you are trying to remember someone's name you might put down the letter you think it begins with, where you last met that person, what he does,

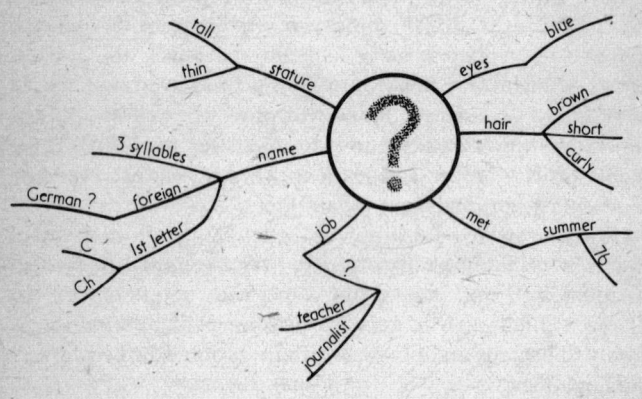

how you first met him, the colour of his eyes and anything else you can remember. While you are doing this you will usually find that the missing fact comes back. If, however, you find that after making all the connections you still cannot remember, leave the pattern for a day and then come back to it. You will find that you recall more surrounding detail the following day and perhaps the missing centre as well.

This technique which allows your mind to dwell on things for a day, or even for several weeks, can also be invaluable in the preparation of any information or with problem solving.

To demonstrate that the more you think and try to remember the more you do actually remember, try writing down all the girls' names you can think of beginning with 'A'. If you repeat this exercise tomorrow you will usually find that you can remember more girls' names beginning with 'A' than you did today. The day after you will remember even more. Once you give your memory a clear direction it continues to work for you while you are attending to other matters. Consciously to strain your memory only hinders rather than helps recall.

Memory and creativity

Creativity is often defined as an ability to relate what previously had not been related. You are being creative when you bring together two pieces of information and create a new whole. If you combine the idea of an egg and a person you might produce the nursery-rhyme character of Humpty Dumpty. For a long time creativity was considered to be the child of the gods — you had to wait for divine inspiration. However, when you have a creative idea you are simply combining in a unique way what already exists.

Most artistic and scientific breakthroughs have depended upon two or more existing pieces of knowledge which one man has combined together to produce a new breakthrough.

151

Creativity is dependent upon memory. The greater a person's store of knowledge and experience the greater tends to be his chances of creating something new from that knowledge.

Tony Buzan has pointed out that memory systems also use a similar creative process; in taking two components, and combining them, in a unique way, you are producing one new idea from two previously unrelated ideas. Memory and creativity are part of a single process.

Memory and imagination

Imagination helps memory by making information more lively. Living knowledge and mnemonics are both ways of making information more lively. Living knowledge and mnemonics are both ways of making information more colourful and real.

Man's imagination enables the sum of his mind to surpass the total of the working parts. When you perceive the world, you experience it through limited senses. These senses only pick up a small spectrum of the stimuli available. However, your memory and imagination give you an internal universe that can be even more magnificent than anything usually perceived.

The brain is divided into two hemispheres, two halves — the left and right. Usually the left controls your speech ability, your powers of logic, arithmetic ability and other analytical abilities. The right hemisphere is more involved with imagination, colour, and creative abilities. The right hemisphere, which tends to be under-used in Western society, and is rarely encouraged in conventional education, is used in mnemonics and whenever you use your imagination to help your memory.

Memory and intelligence

Whereas people do not take excessive offence if they are called

152

unimaginative or uncreative, they will howl if referred to as unintelligent. Intelligence is one of society's favourite yardsticks. Conversationally the word is used to describe anyone, from a polymath through to a neurotic introvert! It is a label which is highly emotive and rarely defined.

One definition of intelligence is that it is a person's ability to make a connection between one idea and another — in other words a person's ability to see how two things relate or differ. Intelligence tests mark a person's ability to compare, contrast, reason, make verbal comparisons, arithmetical computations, test word fluency, perceptual speed and short-term memory. Increasingly these tests are recognised as simply giving a score to a person's ability to do such tests. For example, anyone can practise IQ test technique and as a result dramatically increase their overall score. It follows therefore that the test has not determined a person's innate intelligence but their ability to approach a question in a certain way. In IQ testing and intelligent activity generally to see how things relate or differ, you constantly rely on short term memory and longer term classification and categorisation. Memory therefore plays an integral part in both creativity and intelligence.

Memory and comprehension

All understanding relies upon an active memory. However, short-term memory is limited in capacity to seven or eight bits of information. This can be demonstrated if you try to work out 1,824 x 79 in your head. You will find that it is extremely difficult to hold all the component parts of the problem in your mind at the same time.

Whenever you are faced with a series of ideas to think through, or any situation where you have to consider a lot of different information, first put the information into your long-term memory. Your mind can then work swiftly and easily without imposing a strain on your short-term memory.

Memory helps comprehension by using what you know as a

basis on which to understand anything previously unknown to you. When you explain an idea to someone else it usually helps if you compare whatever you are trying to explain with an idea already understood by the other person, or if you use an analogy or metaphor. In doing this you are making a memory connection easier for them.

Effects of memory development

The effects of improving and directing your memory through the advice given in this book will be as follows: firstly, you reverse the shrinking effect of memory. A tree, once seen and remembered, tends to shrink in your mind as time passes. However, by using the review system you can retain the full colour and splendour of every fact and experience.

The use of 'living knowledge' and mnemonics fires the imagination. You find the increased take-in and storage of information both stimulating and refreshing. You are more able to link up to, and relate to, new information, and therefore find many more areas of knowledge and human experience fascinating. You will improve your level of mental flexibility, tolerance and interest in new ideas.

Realising the effect of pre-set on your memory and performance you can set yourself for information and experience that you want to notice. You can develop your image-memory ability and use the image to give yourself goals and aims that you want to achieve. In fact, one definite self-image you need to give yourself is the image of yourself applying what you have learned from this book. Use the self-image to direct yourself towards new horizons of achievement.

Only recently has man seriously tried to unravel the workings of his own memory and this continuing investigation will constantly enrich and improve man's understanding of himself and of how he experiences the entire world.

Summary

X The evidence suggesting that man may have perfect memory included: 'S'; Penfield's brain research; cues from the environment, like the profile of a face; diaries; recall under hypnosis; truth drugs; death-type experience; dreams; the memory capacity of the brain; the use of memory systems and, finally, the way that the mind will relentlessly search out information once it is given a direction

X The retrieval pattern can be used to remember most information that cannot be immediately recalled

X Creativity is not dependent upon inspiration, it is the combining of existing information in an original way. The creative process is therefore inseparable from memory

X Imagination re-uses stored images. The imaginative ability seems to be controlled by the right hemisphere of the brain

X Intelligence relies on short-term memory and the categories, classifications and store of long-term memory

X Memory makes something new comprehensible by relating old ideas to the new

X Memory is an integral part of man

Further Reading

Specially recommended

Buzan, T. *Use Your Head* (BBC Publications, 1974) This book introduces various methods to improve learning performance. Two chapters are devoted to memory patterns.

Gregg, V. *Human Memory* (Methuen 'Essential Psychology', 1975)

Hunter, I. M. *Memory* (Penguin, 1964)

Luria, A. R. *The Man with a Shattered World* (Jonathan Cape, 1973; Penguin, 1975)

Luria, A. R. *The Mind of a Mnemonist* (Jonathan Cape, 1973; Penguin, 1975)

Bibliography

Adams, J. A. *Human Memory* (McGraw-Hill, 1967)

Bartlett, F. C. *Remembering* (Cambridge University Press, 1932)

Blundell, J. *Physiological Psychology* (Methuen, 1975)

Buzan, T. *Speed Memory* (David & Charles, 1977)

Buzan, T. *Use Your Head* (BBC Publications, 1974) This book introduces various methods to improve learning performance. Two chapters are devoted to memory patterns.

Calder, N. *The Mind of Man* (BBC Publications, 1970)

Coué, E. *Self Mastery Through Conscious Autosuggestion* (Allen & Unwin, 1974)

Gregg, V. *Human Memory* (Methuen 'Essential Psychology', 1975)

Halacy, D. S. Jr. *Man and Memory* (Harper & Row, 1970)

Herbert, F. *Dune* (Victor Gollancz, 1966; New English Library, 1969)

Hilgard, E., Atkinson, R. C. and Atkinson, R. L. *Introduction to Psychology* (Harcourt Brace Javanovich, 6th ed, 1975)

Hunter, I. M. *Memory* (Penguin, 1964)

Jung, C. *Man and his Symbols* (Aldus Books, 1964)

Koestler, A. *The Ghost in the Machine* (Hutchinson, 1967; Picador, 1975)

Lausch, E. *Manipulation* (Aidan Ellis, 1974; Fontana, 1975)

Luria, A. R. *The Man with a Shattered World* (Jonathan Cape, 1973; Penguin, 1975)

Luria, A. R. *The Mind of a Mnemonist* (Jonathan Cape, 1973; Penguin, 1975)

Maltz, M. *Psychocybernetics* (Prentice Hall, 1960; Pocket Books, 1969)

Mueller, C. and Rudolph, M. *Light and Vision* (Time Life Pocket ed, 1969)

Murray, P. and L. *A Dictionary of Art and Artists* (Penguin, 1968)

Ornstein, R. E. *The Psychology of Consciousness* (Jonathan Cape, 1975)

Rose, S. *The Conscious Brain* (Weidenfeld and Nicolson, 1973)

Sheehan, P. W. *The Function and Nature of Imagery* (Academic Press, 1972)

Talland, G. A. *Disorders of Memory and Learning* (Penguin, 1968)

Wilson, J. R. *The Mind* (Time Life Books, 1966)

Yates, F. A. *The Art of Memory* (Routledge and Kegan Paul, 1966; Penguin Books, rev ed, 1970)

Courses

You may be interested to know of Courses run along the lines of this book and details may be obtained by writing to the author, c/o Sphere Books Ltd, 30/32 Gray's Inn Road, London WC1X 8JL.